CHILTERN COUNTRY

The Face of Britain Series

*Uniform with this Volume in Size
and Style*

ENGLISH LAKELAND
By DOREEN WALLACE

COTSWOLD COUNTRY
By H. J. MASSINGHAM

CHILTERN COUNTRY
By H. J. MASSINGHAM

THE HOME COUNTIES
By S. P. B. MAIS

EAST ANGLIA
By DOREEN WALLACE

ENGLISH DOWNLAND
By H. J. MASSINGHAM

SOUTH-EASTERN SURVEY
By RICHARD WYNDHAM

WEST COUNTRY
By C. HENRY WARREN

NORTH COUNTRY
By EDMUND VALE

THE HIGHLANDS OF SCOTLAND
By HUGH QUIGLEY

THE LOWLANDS OF SCOTLAND
By GEORGE SCOTT-MONCRIEFF

THE FACE OF IRELAND
By MICHAEL FLOYD

WELSH BORDER COUNTRY
By P. T. JONES

SHAKESPEARE'S COUNTRY
By JOHN RUSSELL

Published by
B. T. BATSFORD LTD.
15 NORTH AUDLEY STREET, LONDON, W.1
and MALVERN WELLS, WORCESTERSHIRE

I   CHILTERN AUTUMN NEAR TURVILLE

THE FACE OF BRITAIN

CHILTERN COUNTRY

By

H. J. MASSINGHAM

*Illustrated from Photographs,
and from Drawings by*
THOMAS HENNELL

Formosam resonare doces Amaryllida silvas

SECOND EDITION, REVISED

LONDON
B. T. BATSFORD LTD.
15 NORTH AUDLEY STREET, W.1
& MALVERN WELLS, WORCESTERSHIRE

By the Same Author

THE ENGLISH COUNTRYMAN
REMEMBRANCE
ENGLAND AND THE FARMER
THE TREE OF LIFE
WOLD WITHOUT END
DOWNLAND MAN
IN PRAISE OF ENGLAND
THE FRIEND OF SHELLEY
UNTRODDEN WAYS
THROUGH THE WILDERNESS
ENGLISH DOWNLAND
GENIUS OF ENGLAND
COTSWOLD COUNTRY
SHEPHERDS' COUNTRY
THE SPRING OF THE YEAR
THE SWEET OF THE YEAR
AND MANY OTHERS

TO

C. HENRY WARREN

First Published, Autumn, 1940
Second Edition, 1943-4

MADE AND PRINTED IN GREAT BRITAIN
FOR THE PUBLISHERS, B. T. BATSFORD LTD., LONDON
BY MORRISON AND GIBB LTD., TANFIELD, EDINBURGH

PREFACE TO THE SECOND EDITION

I HAVE made no changes in this new edition with the exception of accepting certain minor suggestions and emendations made in reviews and by private correspondents. This, however, should be said. I wrote the book just before the war and constantly urged in its pages the criminal folly of our urban rulers having allowed the entire rural structure of the Chilterns to fall to pieces. The war has entirely justified that criticism, and, though the omens are by no means promising, I can only hope that bitter experience will have taught the Government not to repeat the shameful error of 1920 when the present war is over. Nations have their second and even third chances to retrieve their blunders, but no more.

H. J. M.

July 1943.

PREFACE TO THE FIRST EDITION

S. E. WINBOLT'S *The Chilterns and the Thames Valley* (1932) is, to the best of my knowledge, the only book yet written which covers the Chilterns as a whole, and its scope takes the reader far beyond the area of the Chilterns proper. A heap of county books has included the Buckinghamshire Chilterns, to-day the least interesting section of the range, while the literature of the Hertfordshire and Oxfordshire Chilterns is extremely slender. It seems time, therefore, to write a book on the Chilterns without leaving out or adding on. This I have attempted to do.

Though I have run through a great many books, I have in the end depended upon personal observation throughout. This is not to depreciate the value of the regional books consulted, but for better or worse we are rather tired of the repetition of literary anecdotes and the enumeration of local antiquities dissociated from the life of the people. Accordingly, I hunted for byways literature—agricultural reports, parish records, studies in the distribution of vegetation, annals of country crafts and the like. Among these I would specially mention the monumental work of Drs. A. G. Tansley and G. Claridge Druce, *The Victoria Histories*, Mr. G. Eland's researches into various phases of life in old Buckinghamshire and the authentic local (Bucks) sketches and notes of Mr. H. Harman. To all these I am indebted, though only incidentally. Since only one of the books I consulted touches the Chilterns of Oxon and Herts, I have given the story of the Chilterns as a whole so far as I know them and have seen them, and with only occasional references to any books.

The fashion in guide-books has changed of late years, and much more attention, quite rightly I think, is now given to the geology, topography, agriculture, ecology, crafts, vegetation, village architecture, landscape, flora and ornithology of a given district than it was when the books on the Buckinghamshire Chilterns were written. My own book cannot claim to be exhaustive enough to be called a guide-book, but I have paid due regard to all these elements so far as my personal observation has been able to come into contact with them, without excluding those which readers would be sure to find in the familiar guide-book of the past. The variety of these elements calls for unification and that is the principal reason why my approach to them has been one of personal impression rather than that of an objective report. Lastly, I should mention that I have included in the narrative certain aspects of the more important social changes that have affected the Chilterns and of these their suburban colonization over certain areas is a momentous one. This last phenomenon is either totally ignored in former books or lightly and marginally referred to. Rightly or wrongly I am of opinion that a historical factor of our own times that is generating such profound changes in the social, agricultural and other conditions of these hills should not be regarded as irrelevant to the Chilterns theme.

The reader will notice here and there an occasional repetition. This is deliberate in order to keep the few main lines of the theme knit together.

In conclusion, I would pass a sincere word of thanks to Miss Joan Parry for aiding me when restrictions of transport and personal injury made travelling very difficult, to Miss Garson of the Wycombe R.D.C. for some valuable information about the efforts to save the South from the speculative builder, and last but by no means least to Mr. Harry Batsford himself. He possesses a wonderful knowledge of the English countryside, and his tact in lending unfailing help to his author without pressing it upon him is one reason why he is so successful as a publisher. My friend, Mr. Hennell, I need not thank. He and I have now been associated in three books, he the draughtsman and I the writer, and if he is as happy in the partnership as I am, there is no more to say.

H. J. M.

Summer 1940.

CONTENTS

ACKNOWLEDGMENT

THE Publishers have pleasure in acknowledging their obligation to the following photographers whose work illustrates these pages:

Mr. Harry Batsford, for Figs. 1, 12, 13, 29, 62, 63, 68 and 73.

The Board of Education (Victoria and Albert Museum), for Fig. 22.

Mr. Fred H. Crossley, F.S.A., for Figs. 23–26, 44 and 45.

Mr. J. Dixon-Scott, F.R.P.S., for Figs. 4, 11, 38, 43, 48, 52, 78, 79, 82, 84, 88, 101, 104, 107, 109 and 112.

Messrs. Dorien Leigh Ltd., for Figs. 41, 47 and 102.

Messrs. Eagle Photos, for Figs. 19 and 39.

Mr. Herbert Felton, F.R.P.S., for Figs. 37, 49, 55, 56, 77, 83, 89, 100 and 105.

Mr. Leonard Gayton, for Fig. 103.

Mr. F. A. Girling, for Figs. 3, 14–18, 20, 21, 28, 30–33, 35, 54, 57, 59, 61, 64–67, 69, 71, 72, 74, 75, 86, 87 and 91.

* Mr. Norman Greville, for Fig. 97.

Vera and Humphrey Joel, for Figs. 42, 106 and 111.

Mr. A. F. Kersting, F.R.P.S., for Figs. 46, 50, 51, 80 and 81.

The Mustograph Agency, for Figs. 76 and 95.

Miss Joan Parry, for Figs. 2, 5–8, 9, 10, 53, 58, 60, 70, 92, 93 and 96.

Mr. Staniland Pugh, for Figs. 99 and 108.

Mr. John H. Stone, for Fig. 85.

* Mr. C. E. Sweetland for Figs. 114 and 115.

Mr. Will F. Taylor, for Figs. 34, 36, 98 and 113.

The Times, for Figs. 27, 40, 90 and 110.

Messrs. Raphael Tuck & Co. Ltd., for Fig. 94.

The map endpapers have been specially drawn by Miss Norah Davenport.

* These three photographs were very kindly lent by Mrs. O. Langley-Taylor of the Penn Country branch of the C.P.R.E.

2   LOOKING INTO THE WORMSLEY VALLEY : EARLY SPRING

3 BLUEBELLS IN THE OAKWOOD, SHIRBURN WOOD

CHAPTER

I

INTRODUCTORY

I

THE WOODS AND THE WOODMEN

I AM not going to waste my own and my readers' time by
speculating upon the geographical boundaries of the Chiltern
Hills. All are free to choose their own, and mine will appear in
the text of the chapters to come. Suffice to say here that from a
steepish escarpment in the north and west the chalk forms a
creased shelf or demi-anticline that gradually sinks to the south
and east, that is to say, Londonwards to the Valleys of Colne
and Thames. Most of the roads follow the orientation of this
dip and this easy access has ultimately proved prejudicial to the
distinctive characters of some of the Chiltern country. The Chilterns are a chalk downland and merely a section of the north-
eastern arm that leaves the great nodal boss of Wiltshire south of
Swindon. But this section, though chalk, is self-contained by its
peculiar geological conditions, more varied than in other regions
of downland. Scattered over a breadth of from 15 to 18 miles
there are large areas of reddish brick earth, almost as fertile as
the Upper Greensand, whose boundary is more or less marked
out by the entire course of the Icknield Way from the Thames
Valley to Dunstable. Reading Beds of a stiff marbled clay (also
very productive when properly worked) occupy broad patches
with outliers in the south and east. Gault, studgy London clay,
Thames alluvium, the sandy limestone of Totternhoe Stone, a
clayey chalk marl (admirable for wheat and beans), tertiary
deposits of gravels and clay-with-flints (bearing a luxuriant
vegetation because of its richness in calcium) and pebbly glacial
drifts which form a matrix for the silicate "grey wethers"—all

A

these pockets, patches, outcrops, smears, still further diversify the primal chalk.

The consequences of this multiplicity of soils are, first, a higher ratio of fertility than in other downlands, and, second, a greater variety of natural vegetation. It is quite erroneous to think of the Chilterns as the exclusive kingdom of the beech, which flourishes best on the borders of the inland plateau and down the upper slopes of valleys that branch like trees. Only ash, larch and fir are noticeably infrequent in the mixed woodlands, and this absence of uniformity is of great benefit to the fertility-content of the soil. Another effect, destroyed where urban occupation has occurred, was the wonderful richness and profusion of the flora (5-8), notably in orchises (6-7), mulleins, cranesbills, gentians, Daphne, clematis, wild columbine and certain rarities like coral root, golden saxifrage, *Daphne mezereum*, the Great Pig-Nut, the military orchis, winter green and others, nearly all gone. The Pasque Flower is not, I believe, found in the Chilterns proper, but years ago I saw it blooming on the Hitchin Downs. Hollies, wild gean, the cultivated cherry and the wild box still hold their own, but the juniper (32), older than the most ancient beech-forest, is declining.

The beech, purple in bud, a "glad light grene" in spring and red gold in autumn, makes heavy woodland where the chalk is shallow and the oak accordingly is absent. But the reason is not so much a preference for this type of soil (Tertiary sands, clay-with-flints and glacial drift are also favourable to the growth of beech) as the tendency of the roots to spread horizontally and so combine with the leaf-canopy overhead to deprive other tree-growths of moisture and sustenance, while the beech-litter smothers the tentative sapling. On a deeper soil where the roots are enabled to burrow, the beech is on good terms with neighbours of other species, whitebeam, holly and yew being especially resistant to a beech monopoly. The denser beech-woods occur along the scarp-line but the crowns there are smaller than on the interior plateau where the "bodgers" used to keep the woods adequately thinned. It is generally assumed that a beech-wood invariably makes a bare floor like the nave of a cathedral from which rise the smooth cylindrical columns supporting the carved and traceried and sun-shotten roof. This is an overstatement, because certain plants—wood-sanicle, wood-violet, strawberry, sweet woodruff, archangel, windflower, cuckoo-pint, wood-spurge and, of course, the bluebell on which the pillars stand as though upon a tinted cloud—seize the opportunity of capturing their portions of sun, rain and air before the canopy filters or ex-

4 FRITHSDEN BEECHES, NEAR ASHRIDGE

5   Seedhead, " Jock-go-to-bed-at-noon "   6   Bee Orchid

7   Butterfly Orchid   8   Helleborine

5–8   CHILTERN FLOWERS

cludes them. Of shrub growth the box can survive deep shade where Traveller's Joy would pine and die, while dogwood and wayfaring tree take advantage of clearings, and elder, maple, spindle and hazel front the borders. Hawthorn keeps a strong hold on the gentler beechen slopes of the Middle Chalk; some plants like bird's nest and bird's nest orchis prefer the shaded retreats and green hellebore, the helleborines (8), Solomon's seal and columbine are comfortable in a netted and sifted sunlight. The law of Nature in a Chiltern wood is thus varied and well defined.

But where countrified man preserved the mediæval structure of independent craftsman and small owner, the interplay between him and his natural environment was as mutually beneficial as is the "commensalism" between sheep and starlings. Throughout a large sweep of time, the Chiltern woodlands, especially those of beech, have supported a diverse company of bodgers, woodmen and village craftsmen. At Hedsor, the logs in the Romano-Celtic pile-dwellings were of beech. Underwood coppice, cut every eight or nine years, was used for a variety of purposes. Beech-charcoal provided local fuel, the leaves were used for stuffing beds, the larger trees for bowls, the felloes of waggons (see Defoe), "barn-shovels" and other implements, barn-floors and even house-beams; the medium timber was chosen for the upper parts of chairs; the smallest for chair-legs; the "top and lop" for faggots. The chair-makers by no means confined themselves to the beech, the seats were mainly of elm or cherry and the small market-towns were centres for the harvests of the cherry orchards. The woodmen, carpenters, wheelwrights, hurdle-makers, sawyers and others all had a stake in the land from which they derived their raw material, while the woods themselves were conserved by an inherited woodmanship which considered the quality of the natural wealth no less than that of the products drawn from it.

This balanced economy and interaction has been partially dislocated by the suburban immigration into some portions of the Chilterns as before it by the change-over from the idea of local subsistence to that of commercial expansion, mass-production and the import of foodstuffs and raw materials. When chair-making was industrialized, most of the timber for it was imported from abroad to the loss of health and vigour in the beech-woods. The depopulation of the land was accompanied by the reverse process in the once compact little towns of High Wycombe, Chesham, Rickmansworth, Beaconsfield, Uxbridge, Berkhamsted and others, and the tide of life has shifted from *rus* to *urbs*. Between 1800 and 1900, for instance, the numbers

of the villagers of Ibstone declined from 258 to 116, and this is
a fair average ratio for all the country districts south of the
Oxford-Wycombe-London road and a big under-estimate for
those north of it. Guide-books make little or no reference to this
mutation, though its effects are writ larger upon the Chilterns
than in any other area of equal bulk in all downland. The genus
of woodmen is, in consequence, almost extinct, and the epitaph
on a blacksmith in the churchyard of Nettlebed, copied out by
the enquiring traveller in the Chilterns, Carl Moritz, in 1782,
will in the course of a very few years embrace the entire community of local craftsmen:

> "My sledge and hammer lie declin'd,
> My bellows, too, have lost their wind;
> My fire's extinct, my forge decay'd,
> My coals are spent, my iron's gone,
> My nails are drove; my work is done."

Other rural industries of the Chilterns have suffered the same
doom. Straw-plait and lace-making, once cottage crafts throughout the whole region, have totally disappeared, and no more flax
for the thread in lace-patterns is grown. The making of rush-
baskets and seats for chairs is no more. Oddly enough, I discovered the sole surviving heritage of this most ancient craft—
the earliest pottery was made in imitation of rush-patterns—
not on its hills but in the plain. An Oxfordshire carter still makes
rush seats, and learned the craft in boyhood from a Wycombe
native. Sandstone is no longer quarried; silk-weaving at Tring,
the wool-fair at Marlow, the potteries at Medmenham, Coleshill
and Chalfont St. Peter, the bell-foundries of Little Missenden
and elsewhere, these are hardly a memory. The paper-mills of
Chess, Misbourne and Wye, together with surviving brickworks
and the boot-and-shoe industry of Chesham, have been industrialized, and so severed from their local responsibility and
traditional associations. Though a remnant of bodgers still
supplies chair-legs to the Wycombe factories, machine-turning
has cumulatively reduced the demand for them. The transformation of the surviving Chiltern industries from craftsmanship to
mechanization and subdivision exactly illustrates the saw of an
old Chilterns farmer, recorded by Mr. Eland: "A man as can't
do more'n one thing baint good for anything." If these changes
had been dictated by necessity or had been of benefit to the hills
and their people or the result of a natural process of development
from within, they would, if not welcome nor conducive to the
graces of country or natives, have been acceptable. The contrary
has been true of them.

II

HUSBANDRY AND THE LAND

Apart from woodmanship, agriculture with its attendant crafts
has been the staple industry of the Chilterns from prehistoric to
living times. For this the variety of the soils, the exceptional
fertility of the bottoms and the base of the scarp and the turf-
matting of the tilted sheepwalks are better adapted than are
downs where more uniform geological conditions prevail. The
balanced husbandry of former days pursued mixed farming with
roots, pigs foddered on the beech-mast, sheep folded or at large
on the sheepwalks, and Shorthorns on the hills; the southern
alluvial strip between the Thames and the scarp makes the fattest
land for market-gardening and the rich well-watered western
edging of the Upper Greensand is ideal land for corn rotated with
fodder crops. The Chilterns come or came well into the "wheat-
zone," and the rotation was accordingly based upon the Norfolk
four-course system—wheat, oats, barley and a leguminous seed-
crop folded by sheep. The range thus offered the husbandman as
happy conditions as, with the possible exception of the Vale or
Evesham and the Sussex seaboard, exist anywhere in the South
of England. Cobbett observed of the Chilterns that "chalk at the
bottom with a red tenacious loam on top, with flints, grey on the
outside and dark blue within, is in my opinion the very best
cornland that we have in England." The wheat, he noticed with
that eagle eye of his, grew rather thinly but with full ears. The
hill-wheat rarely indeed yields more than three quarters to the
acre, but is of beautiful quality and the oat crops are as sterling.
Barley, of course, is more at home in the moister climate of the
West. The shelter afforded by the abundant woodlands and
multiple valleys, the comparatively low elevation of the plateau
—none of the hills reaches 900 feet—and the escape of the upland
cherry orchards from the early frosts of the plains, all contributed
to the primeval legacy of a smiling land.

There is plenty of evidence that the farmers of previous eras
made good use of these local gifts of God:

> "Before this strange disease of modern life
> With its sick hurry, its divided aims,
> Its heads o'ertax'd, its palsied hearts, was rife."

The numerous chalk-pits of the hills reveal that the chalk-marling of arable was commonly practised, while a turn-wrest one-way wooden plough of regional design (shorter and lighter than the wooden plough with long beam and mould-board of the Midland clays) was in use both for the steeper slopes and the clay-with-flints. I know a farmer of Weston Turville Mill Farm who used one of these ploughs up to the time when the artificial scarcity of labour forced him against his will to buy a tractor rather than lay his land down to grass. A lightly-built regional waggon with more clearing space than the hoop-raved Woodstock waggon of the plain was skilfully manœuvred upon the inclines. So far as the scanty records go, it also appears that plough-oxen were discontinued at a later date on the Chilterns than in the plain, though the latest record I have is of Great Haseley within sight both of the Chilterns scarp and the Sinodun Hills. A much greater variety of crops, including woad, flax, weld, rye, hemp, lucerne, madder and sainfoin, was grown than in the twentieth century; Black Berkshires thrived and the Hambleden Valley won distinction for its Shorthorns as did the Marlow pastures for the hornless Aberdeen-Angus. Sheep (mostly Lincolns and Oxford Downs nowadays), though never so abundant as on the South Downs, the Cotswolds and in Wiltshire, yet played a full part in the rural economy. In pre-Enclosure days, the numberless heaths of the plateau, some of them extensive, and those with villages upon them probably the sites of the folk-moot, fed the livestock of the open fields village community. It is good evidence for the once great utility of these communal wastes and commons that many Chiltern folk joined Ket's rebellion and, though they are hardly pastured at all nowadays, that the shadow of the old democratic rights is still jealously maintained in various places on the hills. Lastly, the homesteads of local materials, structure and type are homes indeed, snug, compact and roomier than their exteriors suggest.

In no other part of southern England has agriculture declined so precipitously as on the Chilterns. Between 1867 and 1904 the sheep fell off from 349,000 to 178,000 and the pigs from 52,000 to 34,000. Arable, though no exact figures are available, has declined at least from 40 to 25 per cent. of the area, probably a great deal more, since 1800. William James's and Jacob Malcolm's *General View of the Agriculture of the County of Buckingham* stated in 1794 that "in the Chilterns the land is principally arable"; even along the Upper Greensand, a purely arable country, more than half the fields have been grassed down. Since 1904, the process of abandoning the land has been enormously accelerated by partial suburban occupation. These new settlements have been quite

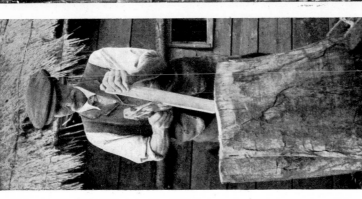

9   A CHAIRMAKER SETS UP THE BACK

10   CHOPPING UP A BILLET

11   TURNING A LEG ON A POLE-LATHE, TURVILLE

12 SWYNCOMBE PARK

13 A BODGER'S SHOP, MAKING TENT PEGS, RUMERHEDGE WOOD,
STOKE ROW

indiscriminate, and the differentiation between rich land and poor land has never entered the heads of builders or settlers. On the contrary, the bottoms and the alluvial strip have been more heavily urbanized than the less fertile summits. Only a handful of Englishmen regard this phenomenon as a tragedy for England, but a truth is not cheated by evading it, and one day by no means in the distant future that tragedy will close, like *Hamlet*, in a harvest of catastrophe.

III

THE UNHISTORIC HILLS

But for the Civil War, the Chilterns of the past enjoyed the privilege of having no history. The towns were all small, the hamlets far outnumbered the villages, the religious of Ashridge, Missenden, Medmenham and Burnham were not large landowners. The churches have their local mannerisms and excellencies but little or no chronicled renown. The heathen Saxons used the Icknield and Thames highways, leaving a barbaric treasure at Taplow, but hardly penetrated the wild and hidden hermitage of the interior. The Danes seem to have swooped into the Fingest Valley and elsewhere, and the Romans sprinkled a fair number of villas in Epicurean places. But the population remained what we absurdly call primitive from the time of the Celtic hill-towns and, likely enough, that of the Neolithic villagers. The fact that outlaws and runaways constantly sought a haven in these hills in later times shows what a byway they were from the miseries of politics and the delusions of progress. The woods and the hills folded in a people content to draw their livings from the earth, their æsthetic skill from the traditions of their fathers and their happiness from their homeland. It is thus that I, its latest recorder, best like to think of this not great nor prideful but very lovable country in the days before the crudities of modern civilization.

The characters of the Chiltern Hills and its natives which I have omitted to touch upon here will not be neglected in the chapters to come. In comparison with other downland landscapes, that of the Chilterns is, as I hope to demonstrate, unique.

II

THE SOUTHERN SCARP

I

THE DOWNLANDS MEET

IF the open-eyed traveller takes his stand on the broad, gently heaving plateau between the Thames and the Chilterns to the west and east and between Wallingford and Streatley to the north and south—say at Icknield Farm or on Coblers Hill or Catsbrain Hill—he is at once conscious of being within the influence of one of the nerve-centres of southern England. I mean real England, the England in which the hills, the vales, the waters, the crops, the roads, the buildings, the natives and the rock that bore them all up on its back were intricately bound together in an organic system not unlike that of the human body.

A mile to the north of Coblers Hill, Grim's Dyke, here banked a little taller than a tall man, throws a green bridge across the large, expressive, open, many-coloured swell of the land between Mongewell Wood, falling like a stream down the south-western slope of the Chilterns, and the cottages of Mongewell, placid by the stream of Thames, like cows at drink. At Foxberry Wood, one of the few islets of woodland in this huge plateau of many-acred arable fields, the Dyke is crossed by the Icknield Way emergent from the woody edge of the hills into this great sea of earth, the old road on its journey from Norfolk to Devon. It has crept along the ankles of the shaggy range, below the trees but above the springs, just where the Upper Greensand borders the chalk, and now a great adventure is before it. It must cross the great fields, like a slow-worm leaving the shelter of a hedge for the open meadow; it must cross the great river and it must sidle along under new downs, the great bare downs of Berkshire that swing off west towards "Phoebus lodging," the ancient Land of

14   CRABTREE FARM, MIDDLE ASSENDON

15　LOOKING OVER THE UPPER ICKNIELD WAY TO THE VALE FROM CROWELL HILL

Desire. The Way responds to the occasion and its manner of so
doing is to put out a series of fibres, like a bramble spray when
it comes into contact with the earth, each of which makes for
a ford of the Thames. One of these is the Papists' Way that
crosses at Little Stoke Ferry and insinuates itself by Lollingdon
Downs along the westerly line of the villages, Aston Tirrold,
Aston Upthorne and Upton where it joins the trunk line over
Hagbourne Hill and as Ickleton Meer continues over the wheat-
shelf that shores up the high wall of the downs to Lockinge,
Wantage and beyond. Another tributary crosses at Wallingford,
that famous place, another farther south between Moulsford and
South Stoke to join the Romanized Port Way, which, as a matter
of fact, is itself, come up from the main crossing at Streatley.

The whole of this region on both sides of the river between
the plain proper and the downland scarp is a maze of tracks and
lanes, like the runways of Hudson's vizcacha communities in
Patagonia. The human traffic was spread over huge heaves of
time. For that reason the discovery of a Bronze Age hoard on
Hagbourne Hill (due west of where I am standing), where
numbers of these tracks, emerging from the river like a migration
of eels, unite as the specific Icknield Way, here a hedgeless cart-
track, is significant of its original age. Mr. Peake accepts that
antiquity as of the Late Bronze Age and so do I. This provisional
dating fits in enchantingly with the origin of the Great Ridgeway
in the Early Bronze Age (*circa* 1800 B.C.), the Saturn and
primordial forbear of all the roads of the western world. The
Icknield Way was of the seed of Abraham, not, as all the books
say, of the Captivity—namely, of the Late Iron Age (100–50 B.C.),
when the Belgæ were preparing the way and forging the chains
for the Romans. The reason the books say this is because the Way
slides in its circuitous fashion under Cymbeline's Mount above his
namesakes, the Kimbles. But if it be granted that Cymbeline the
Road-Maker made the Lower Icknield Way, which traverses the
head of the plain from Ivinghoe to Lewknor, rather than the
parallel Upper Way over the hem of the downland skirt, an
orderly triplication of roads is visualized, as man ventured down
from the hill-tops timidly tapping the wastes of the Vale. No
books have anything to say about the Ridgeway over the Chiltern
Forests, but the supreme patriarch from Avebury and the west
did not stop short at the Goring Gap but flowed on, like the
Great Serpent of myth, over the back of their woody wastes.
Here in this Middle Land where the Chilterns and the Berkshire
Downs begin or end, itself in its slightly raised slightly rumpled
expanse like a creased parchment covered with ancient writing,

B

I can as it were hold the reins of all these roads and ways as though I were a kind of ringmaster. It is so because this open plateau really was the navel of the Midlands on one side and the South on the other in that England which appeared continuously modified but essentially the same between the footing out of the Ridge Way and the Industrial Revolution.

The road-system is by no means the only key. The whole of this great block of country, extending as far as the plain on the north and the two chalk ranges on the south and east and divided by the Thames and its gravels before it turns east at Streatley, is marked by the same characteristics. It is upland, not plain; it mounts gently to the true scarp; though open it is well watered and diversified with coppice and isolated woodland and it is stirred into a low uneven swell. It is dominantly a country of big farms, few hedges, monster fields and arable cultivation. It is a country of sun and wind and of the Jacob's Coat of the crops, at times sumptuous with the play of light and shade. It is something, that is to say, in between the two chalk ranges that are its boundaries, the one densely forested even to-day, the other naked to the sky. It lies in fact between the chalk of the uplands and the gault, Kimmeridge and Oxford Clays of the plain: the clue to it—arable, fruit-farming, streams, lineaments, expression and all—is that it is the country of the Upper Greensand, about the kindest, most generous and comfortable soil to crops and fruits alike that spade or plough could desire. One of the very few regions where lucerne, which requires a deep rich soil, is still grown as a green crop for cattle is on this plateau.

The Icknield Way should indeed be considered the royal road of the Upper Greensand, since it is seldom out of sight of it from Lockinge to Ivinghoe. Nearly the whole of the scarp-ridge from Woodcote and Berins Hill in the south up to Ivinghoe Beacon has its roots planted in this maternal soil, and that is why the old records of the parishes that climb the lower slopes and glide into the plain register a predominance of arable over pasture. It is not so to-day, but to-day does not count in the history of man's intercourse with nature. The Way itself is as often as not the frontier-line of these parishes over the heads of the springs, and we may be sure that it was on the Greensand just below the Way and clear of the hanging woods—the fields under Whiteleaf Cross virtually prove that it was so—that the Bronze Age and Celtic peoples had their cultivated plots and rigs. No doubt the Saxons did too, though the Saxon place-names under the scarp are suspiciously few, and that may be due to their notorious preference for heavy lands, roughly amenable to the eight-oxen plough.

16   THE SOLITARY COTTAGE AT THE HEAD OF THE WORMSLEY VALLEY, FROM WALLACE HILL

17 HARECRAMP FARM, FINGEST, LOOKING TO THE IBSTONE RIDGE

18 TURVILLE GRANGE, TURVILLE HEATH

Thus the rolling plateau pierced by the Thames announces
the junction of the Chilterns with the Berkshire Downs in the
very act of separating them. The two Ways, father of roads on the
crest or just under it, the younger copy parallel with it and
switchbacking along combe-mouth and over spur-tip, carried
on across the Thames and westward together but apart. They
travelled in the same order, at the same comparative elevations
and over the same rock-structure as they had companioned one
another along the line of the Chiltern scarp.

II

WESTERN EDGE

That line of the darkly wooded hills I can see anywhere south
or north of Ipsden, and it is not at all impressive. It is insignificant
until it turns north-east by Swyncombe Downs (29) leaving the
Thames behind and taking the Way with it, tucked away under
the shade of the lowest trees. All you gather, say in autumn,
from this rather mean view of the western scarp from Woodcote
in the south to the Ewelme Downs in the north is a sense of top-
heavy woods tumbling down a bank. This bank is a thin strip of
green between the cumulus masses of the beeches and the long
clean line of fallow or stubble slanting up to meet it. Actually,
the bosses and fingers of tree-clumps in the pastures (especially
those east of North Stoke) advancing into the plateau from the
scarp hold and entertain the eye more persuasively than does the
scarp itself. But this is just as it should be, because the open land
is the bridge between one chalk massif and another, and the
transitional effect would have been compromised if the scarp-
line had been abrupt and bold. No, the woody hills go down on
their knees, as it were, to this great moment in their history,
expressing itself in space rather than in time. This western edge
is a gesture of deference throughout its whole length, and only
those who have failed to look down upon the ocean of billowing
land from the hills as well as looking up at the hills from the
midst of it will call me fanciful. Then you comprehend at a
glance what a great moment it is, the place of meeting and
greeting between the two downlands. As a drama expresses its
most intense or loftiest pitch by especial economy of idiom,
condensation of phrase and packing of the action, so this climax
in the composition of land-masses is made clear to the human
spirit by the opposite. A tremendous expansion and enlargement

takes place on the edge of the confining woodlands, with the shadow-line of the Berkshire Downs as the blue ultimate of the scene.

I know this sun-dappled polychrome stretch of land from various points along the range, and I have a particular reason for choosing that at the back of flint, pepper-potted Nuffield Church. It has nothing in it and is kept locked on the principle of fastening the stable-door after the horse is stolen; but here Grim's Dyke, accompanied by a double line of index beeches down the slope, pushes out plain and full to the eye after a most enigmatic career across the interior tableland. These sentinel beeches flow down the slope in the curves of a kind of crested dragon hauling its interminable length down to the Thames at Mongewell to drink, and the cable is a perfect visual image of the binding together of the wooded ridge to the plateau. Its huge coilings, the swart richly patterned "uplandish" plain, the paps of the Sinodun Hills and the cool cloud-like smoke-blue wave-wall of the Berkshire Downs compose as closely as lines of different lengths and meanings in the same poem. I like this view best in summer, because it is over a field of oats, very weedy but pleasant to the eye since the everlasting pea, lavender and maroon, twines itself among the straw and the bladder campion flowers into more petals than are its due. Mysterious Sinodun to the north-east is a lighthouse in this inland sea of country whose alternating groves and arable and mill-streams give it the appearance of a land of milk and honey. The long dim rampart of the Berkshire Downs catches up the design by displaying its own beech-clumps like bunches of feathers beyond. The greatness of this view lies in the beautiful conformation of the land in which hills and plateau, woodlands and fields interweave their separate identities just as Mercia and Wessex once interlocked their boundaries somewhere over the expanse. Perhaps Grim's Dyke was adopted as that frontier, though much older than the Heptarchy. Along the edges of the rampart just above the ditch, summer reveals glowing drifts of the nettle-leaved bell-flower (*Campanula trachelium*), a stately ornament to the swinging line of the Dyke. And why, I should like to know, is it rimmed about with barbed wire? Hateful at all times, it is a pointed offence aggressively barring access to the Dyke, a historical record of old and far-off things, though they could scarcely have been so unhappy as our own.

The sweep of the eye over a spacious and crowded landscape blends the separate movements of the rhythm, words of the verse, notes of the tune, into a unified impression. So it should

be with the human history of the landscape. Farther south above
Ipsden, where the Drincan streamlet flows down from the
heights, and commons inland replace the dense woods of the
scarp, two narrow combes drive up like a double furrow into
the ridge and leave a wooded tongue of high land behind them.
This is Berins Hill, and succory is abundant along the edge of
the pastures between hill and wood. From the top great rolling
breakers of land are seen to flow up to the breasts of the Sinodun
Hills, and behind the fortified Celtic township on the summit and
the earthworks between it and the river stands the ancient
Dorchester. According to Bede, "the city which is called Dorcis"
was the episcopal see of Birinus who, sent over by Pope Honorius
I. as a missionary, baptized Cynegils, King of Wessex, there in
634. It seems clear that Berins Hill is the mount of Birinus, and
it is nobly fitting that the great physical moment in the geography
of the South Chilterns should thus be paralleled by the great
spiritual moment in the history of man's tenancy of this significant
region. The events of history, too, are reconciled in the single
pattern of those curves and planes below Berins Hill. The busy
traffic along the ancient Ways between 1800 B.C. and A.D. 1800,
the Saxon hunger for wheat-lands, the conversion, the flux of
peoples within the banks of continuity in cultivation create a
mental landscape which springs naturally and harmoniously
out of its physical background.

III

EWELME AND SWYNCOMBE

What Birinus did for this English land is best taken in a
little farther north in the neighbourhood of the Swyncombe
Downs. Here the scarp shakes off its rather beggarly appearance
and rises in something like grandeur, a kind of engraved title-
page to the folio text-sheet spread below. The combe is wider
than at Berins Hill, the slope less steeply pitched and the high
ground, with the long tapering spur of Swyncombe Downs (29)
on the west and the green tree-studded spaces of Swyncombe Park
(12) to the east, is better balanced and more generously composed. Well-informed local opinion considers that Swyncombe
Downs show the best hill-design in the Chilterns, and disencum-
bered headlands are rare enough among these forest uplands to
give weight to that view. The promontory is finely moulded and
aligned, while the Little Cuckoo Pen, the Stranger (the word is

Celtic) Grove on the crest and the scrub and ragwort on its
flank break the austerity of the line and in their due seasons lend
a touch of barbaric colouring to its simplicity. Swyncombe
Downs are something more than minor verse (as the Chilterns
often are), and yet the figuring of the land does not depart from
the Chiltern habit of deep dry combes running into the bowels
of the hills between a system of spurs roughly parallel with the
range more often than at right angles to it.

There is seclusion here, unprofaned by the intrusion of the
present, on the edge of immensity of range in vision; foreground
as well as distance are both in composition, while at no other
point can Sinodun be seen so beautifully gathering together the
whole wide landscape to its breasts. The Saxon-cum-Norman
flint church (35) in the bushy hollow below carries the impress
of Birinus' legacy by round apse, long-and-short work, herringboning and rough blue-and-white flint nuggets of all shapes and
sizes, together with a chancel arch that looks older than the
deeply splayed Norman windows, discreetly filled with green
glass. The aumbry in the chancel, of oak and chestnut, has most
of its original woodwork intact, while the great bell called Jesus
at the west end is possibly a Sanctus Bell and, if so, the largest
known. It seemed to me important to notice the good lettering
of the headstones in the churchyard and the admirable carving
of wings and faces upon them, because an expensively restored
church and a conspicuously up-to-date occupation of the churchyard would have bruised that sense of dear retirement which at
Swyncombe nature and man alike have clothed in beauty. The
Swyncombe Downs are also to be regarded with especial affection
for something else besides the spindle which is locally abundant.
Less than three miles away is the autumnal meeting-ground of
the stone curlew or Norfolk plover which assemble there prior
to migration at the end of the first week in November. Three
pairs nested at an inland sanctuary in 1939 and nearly thirty birds
were present at their traditional common in October. The nesting
pairs are as far as may be protected but with much ado, so
great is the demand for the eggs by that insatiable land-pirate,
the collector. That these noble birds, becoming rarer every year,
should still be nesting in the Chilterns is as good news in its way
as the bare survival of the wood-bodger with his pole-lathe.

Going down the slopes to Ewelme, whose name celebrates
the daylight of a spring, preserves the rare and grateful harmony
of the heights. The downland contours, the autumn furrows
scoring the procreant earth, the swaying waggons carrying
corn, the folded sheep (as seldom seen to-day) (21), the drifts

19   THE CHILTERN LINE ACROSS THE THAMES VALLEY FROM WINTER HILL, COOKHAM DEAN

20 THE YARD, WALLACE HILL FARM, STOKENCHURCH

21. FOLDED SHEEP ON WHITE HILL, A FOOTHILL NEAR IPSDEN

SWYNCOMBE HILL

of snapdragon that old countrymen call Butter and Eggs, the steep
conical ricks, the curvilinear graces of Cow Common (the stolen
village waste), Huntingland and Firebrass Hill, all chime with
the works of man in wayside churches before science, progress,
combines and all their devilments got hold of him. So to find the
Church of Ewelme (27, 22–26) at the foot of those mellow slopes
is the very rose of the journey and draws together as to a jewelled
point all those near beauties of the scene just as Sinodun
magnetizes the flowing spaces of the plateau.

Ewelme is one of the very few thoroughly well-known
churches over the whole area of the Chilterns, so that there needs
no fingering of its glories here. The marvel of it lies not only in
its prodigalities of art, but that they nearly all belong to one
period, the Perpendicular. Beauty is a rarity with us, a lucky
escape; in this church it is as normal and common as black-
berries in the hedge. Flint churches—and most of the Chiltern
churches are of flint—lack the qualities that stone imparts; their
towers and naves always look rather gaunt and rude. But there
is a fair amount of brick-work at Ewelme and the chessboard
arrangement of flint and freestone in the exterior walls—though
not up to the "flushwork" of fifteenth-century East Anglian
churches—yet softens the rigidity and varies the uniformity of
large areas of flint. Since Wingfield Church in Suffolk, containing
flushwork in its walls, was on the ancestral demesne of William
de la Pole, Duke of Suffolk, who built Ewelme Church and the
"howses of almesse" adjoining it, it is more than probable that
the walls of the Chiltern church, built a little later than Wingfield
and unique in all Oxfordshire for this patterning, were built with
the Wingfield model before the masons. Possibly the master
of the works actually came from Wingfield to Ewelme. Besides,
the austerity of the flint makes a perfect setting for the richness and exuberance of the woodwork within—the crocketed
spire and diminishing tiers of arches in the superb font-cover of
1475, the roof of Spanish chestnut covering St John's Chapel
(26), the double tie-beam separating chancel from nave, the
carved wooden figures perched on the shafts of the canopy
(25) over the elaborate tomb of William de la Pole's wife,
the Duchess Alice (22–24), by no means the sainted lady her
pious memorials but not her career of ambitious doubleness
in the Wars of the Roses suggest. What with the old glass in
the east window of the Chapel, mostly of a pale amber in
colour; the excellence of the brasses and stone corbel heads
and of the texture of the encaustic tiles; the gallantry of the
heraldic figures and shields, the happy wayfarer is for once

in a way bewildered with such superabundance of beauty as he would not see from the products in stone, wood and metal of his own age, not if he travelled Europe from end to end. Yet he ought not to consider this church unique, except in the survival of its treasures. He cannot acquire a just notion of the culture of the fifteenth century in England unless his inward eye re-peoples thousands of churches throughout the length and breadth of the land with whole theatres of ideal and realistic figures in wood and stone, now perished from the vandalism of Puritans, Tudor courtiers, restorers and busybodies.

I shall only here pick upon one element of all this lavish and lovely ornament which has not, I believe, been previously noted in print. Glance first at the angels with their curved primaries in the roof of St John's Chapel which has 300 and odd carvings (26). Turn then to the angels in line along the Duchess's tomb, shielded and mailed in golden armour; again to those exquisite ones, also in armour, supporting the stone cushion at the Duchess's head (24), all carved out of a single block, and lastly, to the curly-headed angels of the Duchess's canopy. You can be sure from looking at them all in turn not only that in heaven there are many mansions but many different genera of angels inhabiting them. All these four types—two in wood and two in stone—differ in pose, in expression, in sculpturesque treatment, in wing-shape, in raiment and in the lines and attitudes of the hands. There could hardly be a more telling demonstration of the free-dom of imagination and variety of technique possessed by the old Gothic craftsmen. There is actually another angel-group in the church, pulling a newly-fledged soul out of the earth. This is the decoration of an urn on the south side of the altar, dated 1647. But the angels have lost caste and radiance: they look as though they were beginning to know too much about our muddy world.

The Duchess was, of course, our Chaucer's grand-daughter, and he who loved the wild daisy and the curious ways of man, the most human and natural of our great poets (in spite of his rather Frenchified verse), may serve as the symbol of the unity between the works of Man and Nature along this southern edge of the range within sight of the Thames Valley, the arable shelf and the shadowy further Downs. Sinodun and the green roads, Birinus and the new aspiration of the human spirit, the full flood of that tidal wave at Ewelme, these two are features and limnings of a great landscape, rich in hills and vales and woods. Each landscape, the physical and the spiritual, suggests and worthily represents the other, since the truth of our English country

C

scene, only pieces of which now survive, is that the one was inseparable from the other.

Down the worn stone steps of the covered way at the west end stand the four-square Almshouses in the cloisters, which the Duke and Duchess of Suffolk "set and edified upon a certain ground of ours" in 1448 for the support of two chaplains and thirteen poor men who were given possession of certain lands and a common seal. The scene is one that makes the trespasser upon their peace conjecture whether the approach of death for the old folk is a tearing away from the tranquillity of such an earthly setting or so gentle a prelude to it that its terrors are disarmed. How kind and warm and richly local were these old personal charities, so different from the bureaucratic chill of the moderns! The cobbled court, the carved barge-boards in the central gables of the four cloister porches, the four brick paths leading to the well in the centre of the court, the magpie timbered roof, the oak uprights along the cloisters and the rows of geranium pots between them, the long low pitch of the red-tiled roof with its gabled dormers, the stone mullions and drip-stones of the School, what snugger retreat for old bones? The neat geometrical effect of the whole, so well-ordered and yet serenely bright, is itself a sanctuary from the tossings and anarchy of life without. The place looks like a tiny forecourt of paradise to smooth the grind of poverty and the weariness of age, and only the roar of aeroplanes overhead reminds me that it has drifted down from its moorings in an age when the village community was more or less immune from the rage and riot of the larger world. The ghost of Birinus might well walk these diminutive cloisters, since there is herringboning in them, just as there is in the Saxon churches of Swyncombe and of St. Leonard's at Wallingford.

In the churchyard brooded over by massive elms I could look down upon the red-tiled roofs of the village (27), with the flint walls of the cottages set among gardens full of cottage flowers and fringed by a belt of tall trees. I wondered what could have possessed me to write of Ewelme many years ago as though it were self-conscious and stood upon its dignity. It must have been when I was tainted with Bloomsbury intellectualism and so could see nothing except asquint. This visit was one of repentance, these words are wished as those of reparation. Nor do I know which is the best thing a man may do, come down from Swyncombe to Ewelme or go up from Ewelme to Swyn-combe. Both ways I can take in the disposition of woods, slopes, Downs and their changes in structure as I move, as fine in their

DAME ALICE'S MONUMENT:

24 The head canopy of the effigy   25 A wooden Angel Finial

26 St. John's (the Hospital) Chapel Roof (in the Church)

22, 23 The Monument and effigy of Alice, Duchess of Suffolk, 1475

22–26 CHURCH CRAFTSMANSHIP, EWELME

27 THE VILLAGE OF EWELME FROM NEAR THE SITE OF THE OLD PALACE

The Hospital and School are below the church tower

grander way as the disposition of brick, stone, flint and tile in the
domestic security of the Almshouses. The group of buildings
with the church is in itself a perfect unity and its unity with its
surroundings is manifest, being the full stop to the long lines of
the downland. How consoling to think that this unity between
Man and Nature once existed, that there has been something else
besides the time and civilization of the twentieth century! And if
we look at time as a man on a hill takes in a landscape whose
distances are the past and foreground is the present, we are
comforted by the reflection that it is not man who has failed, but
man at a certain time and in a certain cultural environment. In this
sense, in order to give us perspective and to lighten the burden
of our own period and of its total failure to live up to its heritage,
it may be said that the past lives on in the present. To admit the
failure is an antidote to its poison.

IV

The Face of the Hills

From Swyncombe Downs, at whose feet the Icknield Way
creeps in from the plateau, the range turns north-eastward and
notably increases its loftiness and distinction. The reason is clear:
the low uplands facing the westward-looking scarp are left behind
and the great plain succeeds that marches right into Bedfordshire
on the north-west and, to the north, quite apart from the Vale of
Aylesbury and a few isolated ridges and inconsequent mounts,
includes the whole of the big flat sad weedy pastures of western
and mid-Bucks. The flinty road up Britwell Hill from Britwell
Salome is one of the very few elevated doorways up to the
beechy ridge which is still as it has been for perhaps a thousand
years. In other words, there is nothing incongruous nor unsightly
to jar the experience of going up it. It is full of honest pot-holes
to jar the motorist who attempts it. The start is good, because
the village has many and great trees that cunningly screen at one
angle and reveal at another the shy cottages and bartons of this
sequestered place. The going is good, since along this road in
summer the musk-thistle nods in purple groves and the great
head of *Centaurea* with it. In a wet season, the dusky-yellow
fennel rises to five and six feet, while St. John's wort, harebell,
rosebay, burdock, wild mignonette and the umbel-bearers make
illuminated borders. On one side grow fields of oats, on the other
of barley whose pallid ail casts a subtle pearly glow over the
field. Ragwort, that bright banner of neglect, flows down from

the foothills to meet the corn. The portals open and soon sight is dimmed among the high beechen tops to right and left, but not before it looks behind to view the dark Vale spreading vastly. Britwell, whose patches of flint show the influence of the upland chalk, exactly marks the boundary line between the plain of gault and Oxford Clay and elevations of Portland Beds, and the intermediate Greensand slopes over which passes the Way half-way between the village and the summit of Howe Hill.

If the range from Howe Hill to the promontory of Beacon Hill where it turns a little inwards and again from Beacon Hill to Chinnor Hill (still in Oxfordshire) be regarded at some little distance away in the plain, it presents itself as a solid shaggy wall up to 800 feet without a rift or even a crinkle or so much as an uncertainty anywhere. Actually it is nothing of the kind. On a nearer approach, Beacon Hill (33) advances as the rounded royal bluff it is, powdered with bush and tree; scrub-clothed contours push out from cloudy masses of woodland like a beach sprinkled with drift from the withdrawing tide and a succession of spurs with their corresponding combes and inlets is disclosed like radiating fingers, rather blunt but various in shape and direction. The more southerly stretch, again, is more of a patchwork, blotched with yew and juniper, clear of heavy timber, than the more northerly one, which is as dense with trees as a good wheatfield with straw.

Between Watlington Hill and Christmas Common, one of the tortuous embowered lanes that burrow into the scarp leads to and continues as a footpath below the most remarkable patch of yew-forest that I know. It slopes from the summit half-way down to the dry combe at the base of the hillside, and the contrast between the upper and lower inclines on either side of the path is abrupt. Below the limit of the yews, the ground is naked and quite sterile, the rabbits having destroyed not only all the vegetation except one bird-sown rabbit-impervious elder but the whole of the old sweet nutritious turf of what once was sheepwalk. The slope is now as barren as mountain scree, being nothing but flints and chalk rock. The yew-forest, on the other hand, like a dark cloud resting on the hillside, is dense with young trees that even a dog could not force his way through. No doubt these yews ventured down the hill behind a juniper-screen when the rabbits were much less numerous. All the other scrub that shared in the colonization has gone with the juniper, except a little relict privet, wild rose and whitebeam. The forest is forbidding in the extreme and differs in kind from those of Odstock near Downton and Kingley Vale in West Sussex,

where the trees are of a great antiquity and allow ample room for
ash and other trees. These Chiltern yews are impenetrable even
to rabbits, more so than any primeval jungle, and this black-and-
white hillside is like a heavy frown from lowering eyebrows that
keeps all life at a distance except the plaguy rabbit which has
devastated half of it.

The line is scalloped and nibbled into by many of these dry
combes piercing the base of the hills, and the sweeping bays of
Bald and Beacon Hills (33) are no bad substitute for the rich
contours of the bare downs east of Lewes. The line beyond Beacon
Hill is more uniform, forming a single wide bay between Beacon
and Crowell Hills (15), and their diversity is more to be sought
from the sun splashing over the wooded slopes, especially in spring
when the metallic bright green leaves crowd the delicate branches
like myriads of airy beings settled butterfly-fashion upon them, and
in autumn when these hanging woods are Phœbus' own lodging.
If this section of the range be followed on top, it can be seen at
once how short in the straw are the wheat and oats (though of
good quality) in comparison with those of the Upper Greensand
shelf below, and how much smaller are the fields. The woods too
are more mixed than they appear from below, and the arable is
the clue, since crops are more rarely sown on the shallow soil of
the Middle Chalk that the beech colonizes. Even in deep summer,
the purer beech-woods have great beauty, if none of the radiance
of spring, because the mole-coloured trunks possess a dark rich
velvety glow thrown over them by the shade of the foliage above,
while the sun filtering through patterns the boles in a chequer-
work like tattooing. The land falls away steeply to the plain
(32–33), whose low ridge of Portland Beds between Brill and
Oving appears like a whale asleep on the dark face of the deep.
Here, too, in "a fine and private place," not far from the site of the
old shepherd's grave, the wild lily of the valley still maintains the
memory of a former fairyland. I believe there is no other area of
the Chilterns that is so graced. Christmas Common above the
geometric market-townlet of Watlington is really no more than
fields and woods environing the Fox and Hounds with the pond
in front of it. But the Fox and Hounds with its tiled bow-window,
triangular dormers and walls half-brick and half-flint (31) is a true
type-house of the Chilterns and the Chilterns alone. Flint diffuses
into the plain but not the authentic Chilterns architecture with it.

Here, before the White Mark on Watlington Hill, and, like
Whiteleaf Cross, only just above the Icknield Way, the mind dips,
like Shakespeare's "dive-dapper," into the subaqueous depths of
prehistoric query. Personally, I have small doubt that it is, with

its fellows, the Bledlow and Whiteleaf Crosses, more or less contemporary with the Way itself that is on such close terms with all three. Though I cannot give weighty evidence, still my notion is less flimsy than the customary Danish attribution on no better ground than that one or all commemorate the Battle of Ashdown, which was almost certainly fought on the Berkshire Downs, probably between Lowbury and Lollingdon Downs. The White Mark is a pyramid about 86 feet high and the base 16 feet across, the apex pointing SSE. so that the sun, rising over the hill, possibly at the midsummer equinox, would strike it. This apex of the pyramid, which is remarkably like the ghostly

WATLINGTON WHITE MARK

shadow of a church-spire lying along the hill, ends in a diamond, and it may well be that here is an original pointer to the most potent of the heavenly bodies, from 2000 to 2500 years older than Shakespeare's "shepherds dials." Like Whiteleaf Cross whose base somewhat resembles it in shape though blunter (37), it can be seen, it is said, as far away as from Magdalen Tower. If Whiteleaf Cross is what I believe it to be, an astrological or phallic monument of the Late Bronze Age (and both were intimately linked with the solar cult), Christianized later by a horizontal arm, it is likely that the White Mark was not very much later. Hawthorn, dogwood and the wayfaring tree grow beside it on the sweet-scented turf.

The brief section between Chinnor Hill and Wain Hill ends where the Bledlow Cross, now unscoured among the junipers, is graven on the southern slope and marks the county boundary between Oxon and Bucks. A great eastward-bending arc of the range from Wain Hill takes the Icknield Way with it and the scarp

28 THE UPPER ICKNIELD WAY NEAR THE WARREN
LOOKING TO WAIN HILL

29 SWYNCOMBE DOWNS: THE CUCKOO PEN IS TO THE RIGHT
OF THE PHOTOGRAPH

30   COTTAGES AT IPSDEN ON THE FOOTHILLS

31   THE "FOX AND HOUNDS," CHRISTMAS COMMON, WITH A CHAIR-
TURNING SHED TO RIGHT

between the Cross and Chinnor Hill contains an unmistakable
length of the true patriarchal Ridge Way. It is obliterated elsewhere
by the woodlands, but once no doubt made the crossing at the
Goring Gap to mount up again as the kingly Ridge Way of the
Berkshire Downs. It is only a bit of the tail of the great serpent
along the Warren, but there are two round barrows beside it
and it snakes along in the true manner and position of other
Ridge Ways before it enters the woods near Bledlow Cross.

But the slopes of Chinnor Hill are even more interesting than
the summit. They are very steep and the turf is settled with a
denser congregation of junipers than on any other site known
to me over all the Chilterns. The juniper is the aboriginal bush
of the chalk, and it is probable that these same slopes were bossed
with juniper when the Ridge Way above was worn with hooves
and naked feet. From it falls a green-covered way down to the
Greensand, rich in springs, below, and I infer that this may well
have been a Bronze Age and Celtic cattle-way, studded with
juniper along the high banks then as now, down which passed
Bos longifrons to be watered and pastured on the gentler incline
of the Greensand. Note what is now happening. On the crest to
the left is a beech-wood of youngish trees and these, using the
juniper scrub as a nurse and screen (as the Bantu crouched
behind their massive shields) both against the searing sou'-westers
and the assaults of the desert-making rabbit, are now colonizing
the slopes from the beginning of the fall downwards. Their
trunks are harsh and crooked, not smooth as in the wood, and
they are accompanied by a camp-following of sloe, whitebeam,
wayfaring-tree, spindle, dogwood, buckthorn, bramble and wild
rose that are likewise making use of the juniper as a palisade. In
time, the beech will supplant the juniper and, if the colony
becomes thick and rises to the status of the trees on Wain Hill,
will also become dominant over the rest of the vegetation.

The same process of transformation can be watched on
Pulpit and Coombe Hills farther north, but less perfectly than
on Chinnor Hill. The summit is occupied by fine hawthorns
and, where the slopes of the scarp are gentler, they usually take
the place of the juniper which prefers the steeper gradient.
Chinnor Hill is an ecological close-up of the social history of
the earth's vegetative life on a particular soil and formation
of land-surface. The wanderer on that primeval but changing
hillside is reading a historical novel in which trees and bushes
take the places of men, rabbits and winds of the human environment. Let me not think of that when in October I see these
young beeches of burnished copper side by side with the two

kinds of dusky juniper, one tall, stiff, erect, like organ cacti in
shape, the other low and spreading. The character of this geometrical bush was exquisitely rendered by Leonardo, who loved
and understood Nature as few of his fellow-artists of the Quattro-
cento did, when he placed a juniper as a background to his portrait
of Ginevra de' Benci. When, handling the round plum-bloomed
berries, I look over the plain I can see the smoky-blue fallow
below catching precisely the same tone on an enormous scale,
and, when I walk back through the beech-wood from the thorns
hung with crimson or mahogany berries, I tread a floor of amber.
I read the history of the slope with my mind but I participate in
its pomps of orderly colouring with a sense that is more moment-
ary than the passages of thought but yet is a stake upon eternity.

The villages both of Chinnor and of Bledlow are contained
between the Upper and Lower Icknield Ways, with connecting
roads between them like the rectangular system of a Roman
town. I found Chinnor Church disappointing in spite of the
praises lavished on it by ecclesiologists. The noble structure
with its soaring Early English arch leading from an Early
English nave to a Decorated Chancel is of more intrinsic beauty
than anything Roman that was ever built, but suffers the more by
the clumsy early stone-imitation oak-screen, an imitation pulpit
with imitation ball-flower ornament, imitation pitchpine stalls
and lavatory flooring, not to mention the pedantry, at once
garish and laborious, that models itself in the east window upon
the exquisite north and south windows with their rich deep
greens, blues and ambers like the beech-wood floor. Near at
hand is a foliated cross of 1320, one of the loveliest things to be
seen in all the Chilterns. So outside you see the old headstones
and graveboards deposed from their proper relations to trees,
church and scarp by a riot of rubbishy crosses and gravestones
and the Chinnor Cement Works sticking up against the swing
and dip and rise of the linked hills. Our age for a hundred years
has been rejected alike by beauty and by Nature. It will not
survive their repudiation.

The Upper Greensand, that sweetens the lower slopes up from
the Thames gravels now far away to the south-west, gives a
dramatic exhibition of its generous temper at Bledlow. The
springs yielded by it have scooped out beside the church a gorge
called "the Lyde," deep, sheer and narrow, positively a little
canyon, whose floor beds an appreciable sheet of water that
supports abundant watercress, an old Chilterns industry. The
denser vegetation lower down gives the steep gully quite a
Bryonic appearance, and the higher walls are clutched by the roots

of some grand hornbeams, one of which sends out a fountain of
six trunks, each the girth of a full-grown tree. To walk along
the ravine beside the upper branches of these imperial trees is to
be shot through with a flash of the squirrel's happiness. The sense
of buoyancy combined with the fecundity of the place makes it
the sadder that this fine elemental emotion should be dashed by
the sight of the ivy, whose mats and sneaking trailers swarm over
the branches, blot out the stone walls and what the Victorians
would call "mantle" the slopes that plunge down to the water.
I detest ivy because it is a destructive force only, but still more
the false sentiment that glorifies it. Nothing, I think, betrays
the spurious Victorian taste more than the idealization of this
sinister and dingy plant that weasel-like sucks their power from
the giants of the woods, levels the nobler works of man and
blights his and Nature's creations with the gloom of decay. The
axe is the right approach to ivy, and if it could hew down the
growths of the swampy romanticism that breeds a barren
cynicism no less than an incapacity to distinguish between true
and false, our civilization would not have made the dismal mess
of things it has done.

The ivy disfiguring the Lyde is the more to be regretted when
you come to take in the unsuspected charms of Bledlow Village.
The place rings true, though the lower part is cursed by spots of
the usual planless profit-making building. But the higher bits
up by church and Lyde repay a long look. To begin with, there
is more herringboning in the brick fillings of the timber-framed
cottages than in any other of the Chiltern villages. More thatch
too, and thatch is uncommon on these hills, partly, I think,
because of the short straw of upland crops. There is tile-hanging
as well, and this, though more frequent and workmanly in Kent,
Sussex and Hampshire, does occur here and there in the Chilterns,
if a diligent eye be kept for it. The Red Lion (whence you can
just make out the Cross in a clearing of Wain Hill under its
cloud of trees)—the Red Lion with its whitewashed brick and
russet-tiled roof looks brave against the black weatherboarded
barns (Chiltern style) whose flint-and-brick gable-ends and
flint-cum-brick plinths are typical of the region. The seventeenth-
century Manor with its white dormers in the red roof has lovely
white beading at the eaves (compare it with modern beading!)
like that on the hind-carriage of a hoop-raved waggon. This
shapely elegant building is backed with a fine group of bartons.
The only thing wrong with this end of the village is the ivy
which clambers all over it, street-walls, house-walls, trees. It is a
symbol of progress.

D

I must say a word about the church (34), because fine Chiltern churches are few and far between. The liberty-loving Puritans saw to that, and the restorers rounded off the godly work. There are no fewer than 15 graveboards with carved and moulded newel-posts in the churchyard, and I thought this a record until I found another churchyard in the hills with a score of them. In a general sense, Bledlow was an Early English place, doubtless because the Greensand here gave good living with both hands, and flint flakes and scrapers, possibly Neolithic, turned up in the parish, which also includes a number of the characteristic little Greens—Pitch, Rout's, Forty, Holly and Skittle—which suggest the kindliness of the waters. In a particular sense, the flint church is Early English, harmonising with some fourteenth century features, including a well-proportioned and effective porch, of the sort very rarely mentioned by guide-books. The pillars of the fine door have stiff-leaf capitals, there is a large holy water stoup and a stone sun-dial. The corbel heads under the parapet of the tower are full of character. Inside, you note other excellences besides those proper to the period, like the foliated corbels at the west end, and a modern rood beam and figures placed on the original stone brackets above the chancel arch. Then there is a twelfth-century font with fluted bowl and foliated base and rim—this I mention particularly because, so far as I can gather, this type of font was a local product, and to discover regional flowerings in a specific area like the Chilterns which, architecturally speaking, have homely talents rather than genius, is stimulating. But what pleased me most was a tablet set up by the Guild of Bell-Ringers. "In 1921," it wrote, "in 3 hours and 3 minutes, a peal of doubles, 5040 changes Being 3600 of Grandsire and 1440 of Bob." Follow the names of the ringers. This is grand; it makes the structural beauties of the Early English style alive and significant; it restores to the reader that rich sense of continuity in which his own generation is so pitifully lacking. It was in 1921 that Ophelia's "virgin crants" or paper garlands were worn for virgin burial at Weyhill, once the greatest sheep, cheese and hop fair of southern England and perhaps the oldest fair in the land. To preserve these things in memory is not merely to raise ghosts: it is a hint to posterity when it starts clearing away the rubbish of our own age.

Here at Bledlow I have fixed the end of the southern scarp-line. From outside the village you see a mighty crescent of the range from Cymbeline's Mount in the north to Whiteleaf, Windsor, Lodge and Wain Hills to the east and south. Tumuli stud the cliffs of the bay and both the Crosses hang above gaps in the hills. Bledlow makes a good tail-piece.

32 THE VALE ABOVE LEWKNOR, WITH A DWARF JUNIPER FOREST

33 LOOKING TO BEACON HILL FROM BALD HILL

SOUTHERN ESCARPMENT VIEWS

34 BLEDLOW CHURCH FROM THE SOUTH-EAST

35   THE SAXON-NORMAN CHURCH, SWYNCOMBE,
FROM THE NORTH-EAST

III

THE NORTHERN SCARP

I

ANCIENT WHITELEAF

THE northern scarp of the Chilterns is much better known than the southern—it is nearer the Wen. You realize that from the summit of Whiteleaf whence you can see both the Risboroughs, Monks and Princes, and that nowadays is, as the poet said, all ye need to know. The view offers crudely opposed and incongruous impressions (40). The gentle gradients of the foothills and a sizable area of the plain are just Suburbia, detached from all other cultures, detached from everything—earth, design, tradition, order, meaning, strangely anomalous and fancy-free. What is left of the village (hidden from the Cross) is traditional seventeenth-century Gothic with the customary red-tiling for the roofs and the ingenious mix-up of flint with brick which is the Chilterns. The same materials spread to the Vale but the combinations are different. The Chilterns possessed a genuine architectural mannerism of their own.

Little Monks Risborough Church with its painted rood-screen hides itself from the sprawl of villas. Nor does the eye pick out the pretty arcaded wool market-house of Princes Risborough nor the brick fronts of the Georgian houses near it (38). It is the new Roman Catholic Church which quite dominates the Risborough Gap, a kind of mosque in good red brick clustered with rounded apses in Greco-Byzantine style, of the Basilica type and so true to that of the earliest English churches built by Augustine at Canterbury. I find it an admirable building, and it is appropriate to its place, since Monks Risborough takes its name from Augustine's monks at Canterbury of which it was a cell. Go back a little farther and to the south-west lies the site of the Romano-Celtic

Villa at Saunderton on an outcrop of the Lower Chalk close to
the spring-line, like the Upper Icknield Way within half a mile
of it. The wall-footings were built of the harder "clunch" (as is
the little sixteenth-century dovecot at Monks Risborough) and
the big flint nodules (as in the walls of Reculver in Kent) from
the Upper Chalk of the heights, together with that pinky-brown
siliceous sandstone from the Reading Beds I mentioned in the
first chapter. There are not many scholars of English landscape
who know that the Chilterns quarried their own Sarsen stones
like the Wiltshire Downs (p. 84). This Villa had drying-floors for
the harvested grain, it had foundation burials that take one back
to Merlin's day, but what is more to the present point, its community quite possibly dug chalk marl for manure, as the Celtic
farmers undoubtedly did, and all honest husbandmen up to the
Enclosures and Coke of Norfolk, who revived the good practice,
and the big arable farmers of the nineteenth century, until
"scientific agriculture" abolished it with its earth-flogging
artificials.

The Romans come into the story along this section and from
their little province rises the Cross above the Icknield Way, 50 feet
high by 25 long, from a pyramidal base (Bledlow Cross has none)
340 feet wide (37). It can be seen from Shotover and many a
point in the Vale, just as the White Horse can from Faringdon
Folly and many a point in the Vale. The Sinodun Hills are visible
from Whiteleaf and the blue veil of the Berkshire Downs as
though let down from heaven. The Cross saw and was meant to
be seen with the range of the falcon. As I argued in a book written
some years ago, it has stood or rather leaned against the bluff
above the Way from the time when tin ingots on men's shoulders,
flint from the factories at Grime's Graves, wool-tods on pack-
horses, sheep, cattle and ponies, chapmen and pedlars, pilgrims
and soldiery passed along the Ridge Way on the summit, first as
a solar or phallic sign and from the eighteenth century onwards
as a cross. On the crest of the hill stands a round barrow (shame-
lessly mutilated by its recent excavators) containing burials and
what the archæologists in their deadly lingo call "grave-goods,"
proper to long barrows. I do not suggest that the Cross a few
yards away is Neolithic (2000 B.C.), but I do that it is probably
more or less contemporary with the White Horse of Uffington,
the Long Man of Wilmington and the phallic Helith of Cerne
Abbas. Close by to the south Grim's Dyke approaches the scarp.
The alignment here from the Cross to the earthworks on Pulpit
Hill to the barrows on Five Knolls Hill, Dunstable, and on to
Ravensburgh Castle is significant. At any rate, the immensities

LOOKING TOWARDS MONKS RISBOROUGH

in space to be gleaned by the eye from Whiteleaf are blended
in the mind with the immensities of time, and that is the way
to appreciate landscape.

But that is not all. Behind these successive cultures—prehistoric, Romano-Celtic, Saxon, mediæval, Georgian and the
anarchic pseudo-culture of to-day—is primeval nature. Our idea
of the Chilterns as a domestic downland lacking the wildness
and aloofness of other downlands has here to be modified. The
land with many exultant curves (did the Celts get their curvilinear
designs from their intimacy with the chalk downs?) sheers down

AT WHITELEAF

to a narrow combe from which it rises like a swallow from the
surface of a pond in wooded slopes towards Little Hampden.
Beeches are scattered all over the falling hill, not as woodland but
a scrub, intermixed with a few thorns and their feet clothed in
sweet turf and long grasses. The scene is wholly incult and man-
less, reminding me, if man comes into it at all, of the times when
the Chilterns were a refuge for the hunted and the outlaw—of
petty Saxon kings driven out of their kingdoms by some palace
intrigue, of desperate Cymry evicted from their lands, of Christian
saints and heroes raising obstinate prayers in beechen cathedrals
safe from the Danes, of unsung Robin Hoods harried into a feral
life by the Norman and Angevin game-laws, of open-field

36 IVINGHOE BEACON FROM THE NORTH : A Windy Spring Day

37 THE WHITELEAF CROSS, PRINCES RISBOROUGH

38   THE GEORGIAN MANOR-HOUSE, PRINCES RISBOROUGH, FROM THE CHURCHYARD

husbandmen forced into vagabondage by the Tudor "Inclosiers" and urban speculators in sheep-runs. "Here if you beat a bush, it's odds you'd start a thief," says the *Polyolbion*, and Gallows Hill near Ellesborough and Hang Hill near Drayton are the marginal comment on Drayton's line.

To drop only a few feet down these slopes at the back of the Cross is what Charles Lamb called "a sweet reversion" into reconciliation with a free and unspotted nature unknown to modern man except as a spectacle or a picnic site. Here stoat, rabbit and adder pursue their ancient ways; harebell, field campanula, bedstraw, thyme and St. John's wort are unmolested natives, and here too grows, in single plants as is usual with this member of the orchidaceous group, the patterned spires of *Epipactis latifolia* with its green bracts and white and purplish pink flowers climbing up the stem. It is to be enjoyed, this draught of intimate nature, by contrast with the naked hill-top view of the plain from above the Cross (40)—and more than the plain, since it includes the Corallian heights round Oxford, the Portland Beds ridges to the east of them, the chalk Sinoduns to the south and, as I say, the Berkshire Downs beyond.

The backdoor to Whiteleaf is also "a fine and private place" to see the beech in juxtaposed variations. The first of these is the close-up of massed foliage seen from above and along a gradient. Not a vulture flying on motionless pinions above the Amazon forests could have a happier view of tree-tops compacted into one roof than here on our own Chilterns. Then there is the grove-form, not man-made but natural, as are some of the groves on the Wiltshire Downs. There is a certain formality in this leafy disposition well-suited to the Neolithic barrow whose builders practised a kind of ritual Druidism 1500 years before the so-called Druids. Then there is a striking variety of tree-shapes. Beech seldom varies: the smooth, straight, severe classical column, breaking into a fountain of foliage high up is character-istic of it in all regions. But here there are three other forms. Dwarf beech on the crest exposed to the full onset of the sou'-westers make up in width and density of foliage for what they lack in height; these wind-raked pigmies are mushroom-shaped like dwarf oak growing where there is no great depth of clay. The fasciated form is to be seen just below the crest and several of the trees have a dozen or more trunks. The third form occurs in the woodland to the south of the Cross. Here the trees grow bunched with slender boles and crooked and irregular in shape. This is a sure sign of fairly recent colonization from the summit. This multiformity, the wildness of the scene, the height, the

freedom, the complexity of the slopes, the contiguity of open
boisterous down to a religious shade make the adventure of
Whiteleaf (out of holiday time) as enlivening as any on these
downs.

II

PULPIT HILL

Pulpit Hill, a bluff taking the weight of the range in the same
manner as do Wain and Beacon Hills, bastions the Risborough
Gap opposite Whiteleaf; Cymbeline's Mount is the newel-post
to the range turning east once more and Ellesborough faces the
Wendover group of headlands, all over 800 feet. Let not the
varnish of publicity cover up their primal nobility. There are
earthworks on Pulpit Hill, possible hut floors and a motte-cum-
bailey on the Mount, together with a tradition that Cymbeline's
sons were killed on it in defending the Chilterns against the
Roman aggression under Aulus Plautius. Little Kimble Church

"OPENING" A CORNFIELD

has good murals and some thirteenth-century tiles, and between
it and Beacon Hill No. 2 the Velvet Lawn, Silver Spring and
Happy Valleys make niches in the range. The virtue of this
region is indeed the contrast between the thrust of the bare
bluffs from the Mount to Bacombe Hill and the Tennysonian
(none the worse for that) swards and bottoms curling up to the
trees that come flocking down to meet them. The wild box is
abundant about this wide saucer of rich Upper Greensand under
the chalk headlands. The glides of the lower slopes and the
porpoise-like disportings of the promontories are happily
displayed on Pulpit Hill, and even the great woods hereabouts
seem to roll and rear and arch as in Shakespeare's terrific description of a high-running sea. In the woody pass over Pulpit Hill I
once saw (near where the copper beeches stand) a gyppoes' red
van like the covered waggon of romance. It gave a keen point
to the spaciousness of the scene. But the varnish is about here
all right as well as the timeless oak beneath it.

Ellesborough's flint church, mostly fifteenth century, is
grandly poised on a chalk outlier of the billowy semicircle of

E

headlands (41) and has a graceful lantern at the entrance to
the churchyard. What a difference good placing makes to man's
works! But the Church has been wickedly vulgarized inside, and
the Croke monument, much more chastened than is usual with
Renaissance tombs, looks as out of place in it as would a piece of
old furniture in the Tottenham Court Road. He does well who
stops at the door and takes a good look at the long spur of Coombe
Hill (850 feet) to the east, Beacon Hill and the smooth pate of the
Mount. The By-Pass Variegated style lies ahead, but let him not
miss the excellent bit of thatching at the foot of the church-mound.
This came from the long straws of the Greensand crops, not the
short straw of those of the Upper Chalk. Wendover still possesses
that rich curve of the Icknield Way round into the Aylesbury Road,
its secretive alleyways, the colour-washes, roughcast, red brick and
tiling of its prim and proper little Georgian houses, stray flecks
of thatch, two timbered barns with brick fillings at Wellwick
Farm and the down-and-out windmill of brick, conical-topped
on a conical base, not unlike the more imposing one at Quainton,
east of Brill. Stevenson in 1875 called Wendover "a straggling
purposeless sort of place" sixty years before it became so. In
spite of the environs of this beleaguered little township—they
encompass it like the hosts of the Paynim and the Red Lion
might as well come down as look as it does now—there are still
deep lanes up by Aston Hill and the road itself is the highest in
the Chilterns. Thence the tongues of the spurs, the converging
lateral valleys and the oceanic plain can be seen if care is taken to
prevent the bungalows sticking like styes in the eye.

North-east of the Wendover Gap the Upper Icknield Way
suffered the indignity of having Akeman Street imposed on top
of it and the arterial London road from Aylesbury on top of
that. Nothing more clearly reveals the absurdity of reckoning
history in terms of material progress (still more ridiculously
taken to be inevitable) instead of in terms of cultural profit and
loss. The fusion of these three roads west of Tring, Celtic or
Bronze Age, Roman and our own, shows the compatibility of
the second with the third, both urban civilizations, and the
incompatibility of the first essentially a rural culture with either
of them. The natural freedom of the prehistoric road, self-
disciplined by its adaptation to the mouldings and innate features
of the land-surface, is crushed by the ramrod ideas of the Roman
and industrial ages that, being urban only, seek and sought to
impose their wills upon Nature. The different road-systems of all
four periods (taking in the Saxon) unequivocally declare the
natural affinity between the Celtic and Saxon cultures (both rural)

39   A PLEASANT OLD CORNER IN PRINCES RISBOROUGH

40 LOOKING ACROSS THE RISBOROUGH GAP FROM WHITELEAF
Note hill-foot suburbanization

41 THE VALE OF AYLESBURY FROM CYMBELINE'S MOUNT,
WITH ELLESBOROUGH CHURCH BELOW

and between the Roman and industrial (both urban) together with the fundamental disharmony between the one pair and the other. But this is not perceived because modern education has taught us to read history as a mechanized science and not as the interplay of cultural forces.

Tring was once a straw-plaiting village and Austin used to supply the Vale with the straw-splitting "engines" (four-inch wands of wood with pieces of bullock's leg carved into fans and a point at right angles to the shafts), four specimens of which I have in my museum. Down to it the Roman-arterial road goose-steps, while the Way side-slips to the left. Cobbett, paying a visit to Tring, was shown three bundles of straw from Tuscany for plaiting. Why, he asked, was it not grown and bleached at Tring?—and he pointed to the poverty of the farmers and the acute distress of the labouring folk. There is more true Chiltern history in that gesture and that question of the great Englishman who possessed a genius for looking into the future than can be found in any guide-book. Straw-plait was killed partly by mechanization and partly by foreign importation of shoddy. What the old peasant art was like—it was universal in the Chilterns—may be measured by specimens of sixteen different patterns in differently coloured straws done for me through the agency of Mr. C. Henry Warren by an old lady of ninety-one. The work is of the most exquisite finish, delicacy and lustre, and the murder of it by economic ambition or, in plainer terms, lust for wealth, was not the least of the crimes of the late nineteenth century.

As the old Way slips north again as "the hollow way," shaking off its strait waistcoat, so the wide and woody crescent of the range, deployed in a series of terraced dips, swings round to meet it. At Drayton Beauchamp, the melancholy plain of Beds lies on the left hand, the skipping little hills of Herts on the other side of the scarp to the right and the downlandish ridge of Ivinghoe and Dunstable ahead. Drayton is a sterile-looking hamlet to-day, and the forlorn windmill, similar in structure to the Wendover one, looks sadly down on it. It seems to be thinking of the days when the old squire provided all the cottages with gardens, when the ale was home-brewed, the harvest home an annual festa and five shearers were present on Sheep-Shearing Day. On St. Stephen's Day, the rector was expected to give "as much bread and cheese and ale as the inhabitants chose," but the Charity Commissioners, realizing that the old saw about charity beginning at home had become old fashioned, abolished "Stephening" in 1827. The men of Drayton went on singing,

"My name is Jim, the carter lad, a jolly chap am I, I always am contented be the weather wet or dry" for some years after until their voices died away. There are no harvest homes now because there is no corn; there is no straw-plaiting because there is no corn; there are no markets at Tring and Ivinghoe to take the "scores" of "whipcord," "feather" or "pearl" because there is no corn, and there are no husbandmen, only five cowmen on three farms. The arterial road has won.

III

DUNSTABLE DOWNS

The Lower Icknield Way, whose junction with the Upper is at Ivinghoe, crosses the Grand Junction Canal by a pack-horse bridge at Marsworth. From here the Beacon can be seen looking down its nose at the huge stretches of undulant land below it. The traveller realizes at once that he is in new country, totally unlike any he has passed since leaving the south and reminding him somewhat of the great plateau at Ipsden by the Thames, except that the scarp-line is now nearly all bare downs. The conical shapes of the hills and the indented line of the ridge from Pitstone Hill to the Beacon and again along Five Knolls Hill overlooking Dunstable are curious rather than beautiful. But they are much nearer primordial downland in appearance, though nothing like so grand in mass, height or contour as the inspired lines of the chalk in Wiltshire, Berkshire and the South. They are spacious but in an odd way forbidding, devoid of the homeliness of the Hertfordshire country over the crest but not really elemental. Nevertheless, this section of the ridge points to far horizons as it does nowhere else, since down south it is the plateau which wings the mind, not the wooded scarp. Everything here spells end (or beginning) just as it did by Thames, while the physical appearance of the country once again suggests that a geographical nerve-centre was likewise a human cult-centre.

The numerous outliers; the surge of the plateau, seamed with combes and pitted with depressions; the churches on their mounds in the midst of the generous tableland; the clean scoring of the ridge against the sky; the scene of the meeting of the two Ways, of three counties and of the Chilterns with the watershed of the Upper Thames; the source of the Ouse—all contribute to the pivotal sense. The Ridge Way reappears under the sky on Five

Knolls Hill, where the tumuli stand in a chain as at Stonehenge and Avebury. There are barrows on the west side of Bledlow Down, on Lodge Hill and Whiteleaf, above Wendover, on Ivinghoe Beacon and in Hampden Park, but nowhere on the Chilterns are they conspicuous as on the Dunstable Downs. Lynchets or cultivation terraces, much sharper than at Chesham and West Wycombe, furrow the flank of Cheddington Hill, one of the outliers (43). In spite of O. G. S. Crawford, it is possible to demonstrate by analogy with those of very much harder strata, that they are almost certainly pre-Saxon, and they are a perfect example of the difference between prehistoric and modern slope-cultivation. Terraces conserve the moisture and retain the humus. Our scientific ideas, contemptuous of the old balanced peasant economy and respect for the soil, drag crops out of it by forcing and by monoculture, with the result not only of soil exhaustion but on the slopes of sheet erosion, the worst form.

At Totternhoe, another outlier, Norman earthworks were built up on what was probably an Iron Age Camp; at Maiden Bower, yet another, is an authentic Neolithic Camp. At Eaton Bray, there is a tithe barn, one of the very few in Beds, and at Edlesborough (Bucks) another, early Tudor and of brick within a timber framing. There are also two fine "stirrup-shaped" moats at Edlesborough and Pitstone and a seventeenth-century dovecot of brick and timber at Edlesborough. A century ago, this region was a lively centre of straw-plait, Dunstable being not only a market, like Tring, but having a close-woven "whipcord" pattern of its own called "Dunstable Plait." The complex stratification of cultures, each one leaving its own signature to swell the total impression of man's continuous and creative intercourse with the earth, is set off by an addition to the natural strata of the underlying rock—the Totternhoe Stone, used abundantly in the quoining and framing of the church walls. Here too, the Upper Greensand, spread over the plateau, thins and finally peters out to the studgy Gault. And in Dunstable itself, the Icknield Way is cloven in two by Watling Street. Is not this region Finis or Overture to the Chiltern Hills?

The churches of Ivinghoe and Edlesborough are not the least of the contributions to the landscape. They are both lofted, as at Ellesborough, on massy mounds, possibly artificial in origin, and both have high flint towers whose beacons balance Beacon Hill. Ivinghoe's "faire church of Our Ladie," with a rather foolish leaded spirelet as at Hemel Hempstead, is happily placed at the end of a line of rowans, whose bright berries in autumn are like a peal of bells, just at the point between the open and curving little town and the open plateau where migratory birds flock at the fall of the year and lapwings and starlings make communal and intricate flights at the close of the day. A mere inventory of the good things in the church rolls back the centuries—Rabelaisian corbel heads of stone to the open timber roof, an oak lectern, fine poppy-heads with bold rough carving and masks in the middle of the fleurs-de-lis, an ornate and canopied Jacobean pulpit with an hour-glass supported within ball-turned framing at the end of a rod (46), Decorated windows of an unusual design and others. But when you add to these what the restorers of 1871 *removed*—namely, a thirteenth-century font and rood-screen, a fifteenth-century window, a fourteenth-century brass, three altar-tombs, the armorial parapet to the west front and two porches—you realize that to-day we very rarely see anything but fragments of the beauty of the past and that the Industrial Revolution piled up the wealth of the nation at the cost of beggaring its creative powers and robbing it of what those powers had once produced. But I think that the original builders made a mistake with the Totternhoe Stone. It weathers and flakes so badly that the exterior where it is used with the flint looks as though it were smitten with dermatitis.

Edlesborough Church on an even loftier mound poises farther north across one of the deep combes with which this country is riven, and commands a brave view of the downs etched against the sky, scarred with quarries and pocked with disused chalk-pits like gigantic bird-droppings. From the church too the Whipsnade Lion is obtrusive in its naturalistic form against the hillside. What a pity that the designer failed to note that the great original of all the chalk figures on the downs—the White Horse of Uffington—is *stylized*, as all such figures should be, not magnified copies out of a picture-book. They knew better how to do these things in the ages B.C. On the mound, yews, chestnuts and sycamores take off from the bleakness of the site without compromising its dignity. The interior was once even more splendid than Ivinghoe's, full of that magnificence, simple piety, caricature, satire, fantasy, realism, poetry, extravaganza, which the old wood- and stone-carvers lumped together in the sacred building with incongruity only to the fool who says Shakespeare should never have brought the Porter scene into *Macbeth*. That was the marvel of their art, their intuitive understanding that in heaven there are many mansions. The fifteenth-century masons and wood-workers cared nothing that the wonderful pulpit

42 CHALK RAMPARTS AND WIDE STRETCHES, NEAR EDLESBOROUGH

43   VIEW LOOKING NORTHWARD FROM IVINGHOE BEACON TO EDLESBOROUGH CHURCH

canopy (44), carrying refinement in structure almost to excess, should be a few yards away from the crude and comic turns of the misericords in the choir, one of which (among the Edward Lear wonder-beasts) shows a lion drinking at a mermaid's breast. No, the prodigality of Nature's forms was worthily answered by that of the carvers in mood, theme and treatment.

That is why the spirits drop to zero when you come out of the church and look at the monstrous sprawl of new buildings all over that kind and fertile soil between church and downs. What has happened to us that, a few centuries after those builders and craftsmen could do nothing wrong with their buildings, we can do nothing right with ours? It is desolating that there was nothing they touched but they enriched, and nothing we touch on the face of the earth but we deface. Anybody can see for himself that, though our churches belong to five centuries, often mixed up in one of them, yet the artistic tradition was not snapped, and that even after the Reformation the Gothic tradition in wood-carving (witness the octagonal "wine-glass" pulpit at Edlesborough (45) was maintained. It is about time that social historians paid some attention to the break in the tradition of craftsmanship and fine building which stepping inside and outside this church porch reveals as with Bunyan's "spectacles of observation."

The second biggest break in the downland range between the Marlborough Downs and the Wash occurs here among the head-waters of the Ouse, and here, therefore, I propose to halt. I started from one of the nerve-centres of the South and I stop at one of the nerve-centres of the Midlands. Down the smooth slopes of the Dunstable Downs they used to roll oranges for the people to scramble for at the bottom, just as they used to roll cheeses down the mighty slopes of White Horse Hill. Here my rolling stone comes to rest.

IV

THE SOUTH

I

SOUTHERN SHORE

THE shore-line along the southern edge of the hills to the east of Medmenham right away to Burnham Beeches and Farnham Royal is to be called the Chilterns nowadays only as a discourtesy title, though a friend would have me qualify this by pointing out there are tracts of wide fresh woods, open commons, secluded lands and quiet primitive dwellings in the flatter sandier tracts round Hedgerley and Fulmer. A country-loving local motorist once showed him how to thread his way from Slough to Gerrards Cross through extremely rural byways every step of the run—but is this lower gently heaving country of birch and heath to be really reckoned among the Chilterns? Both Marlow and Henley have kept pieces of their Georgian past that in respect of scale and materials come within the fold of Chiltern architecture, especially Henley. But if their backs are to the hills, their fronts are to the water and they are or rather were riverside market-towns.

The least modernized region of the riverfront is Bisham Church and Manor (48), the latter invisible. The interior of the church contains remarkable Renaissance monuments of the Hoby family, kneeling figures on one tomb (50), sham reclining knights on another (51) which for their diverting complacence and pomposity remind me of the Fettiplace tombs at Swynbrook in the Oxfordshire Cotswolds. St. Peter must have welcomed those Elizabethan Hobys with an angelic band and a seraphic guard of honour. The churchyard on the edge of the water (it has graveboards as at Bledlow) is a moment of serenity and quiet breath, while across the storied river rise the wooded hills of Hambleden to the

44, 45 THE SOUNDING BOARD AND
PULPIT, EDLESBOROUGH CHURCH

46 THE PULPIT HOUR GLASS
47 THE SOUTH PORCH
IVINGHOE CHURCH

48   BISHAM ABBEY BY THE THAMES

49   THE DOG AND BADGER INN, MEDMENHAM

north. For a split second a Hoby masque on the broad chest of
old Father Thames stirs like "a little noiseless noise among the
leaves." Bray has crumbs of itself, and from the Quarry Woods,
where still the wild daffodils slow the swift foot of Proserpine,
there is a view down into the river valley that has the curious
mixture of the great and the commonplace to be seen in the
naturalistic water-colours of David Cox. But though Cliveden
still remains it is muffled up in its own woods and the way to
see it is not from this coast but the hills above Marlow. Between
Bourne End and Loudwater along the course of Wycombe's
Wye (83) you pass from the shabby-genteel to the naked
industrialism which changes its name to Styx. Most of the rest
of the space between Marlow and Slough is nowhere. It has no
identity, no meaning, no reality. It is like a dream after a supper
of lobster and roast duck.

For some reason, possibly the terror of public playgrounds, I
had never been to Burnham Beeches before 1939 and knew of
them only from Gray's letter to Walpole: "Both vale and hill are
covered with most venerable beeches and other reverend
vegetables that, like most other ancient people, are always
dreaming out their old stories to the winds." When I did go out
of conscience to this book, I was bewildered by the utter incongruity of that sentimental impression. Whatever they are,
they are not like old cronies dreaming before the fire. Whatever
they are, they are one of the wonders of the world. Not all are
beeches—there are elms and birches too and hoary hollies that
blaze with jewels in autumn—but all belong to the same mysterious fraternity. I have a great affection and reverence for old trees
—together with some knowledge of the great ones of the Midlands and the South—but this patriarchal company was something new to my experience. Patriarchal?—prediluvian rather.
Actually the beech is one of the youngest of our native trees, and
it is doubtful whether it began to colonize the Chilterns much
before 3000 B.C. between the Atlantic and sub-Boreal (dryer)
periods of geo-chronology. Nor in all probability—so far as
pollen analysis is a guide—did it reach the plateau from the scarp
until Saxon times when the upland arable was left derelict. But
these Burnham trees look older than man himself.

Most of them are pollarded and so more or less fasciated for
the sake of keeping the life in them. Their arms are thus very
thin in proportion to the enormous, the fabulous girth of the
trunks (52). None of them are whole and entire. They are
pierced with cavernous holes or rent into vertical crevices or
yawning with tenebrous chambers between roots and bole or

F

severed as willows so often are nowadays for lack of cutting the withies. To maintain the slow, ponderous, primordial life in themselves, they have agonized their woody, stunted, massive torsos into incredibly serpentine and elephantine shapes; they have swollen out into warted and bulbous excrescences and they have pushed huge pachyderm roots which grasp the soil like a boa-constrictor wound about a stump or like a mammoth planting down its foot. A suburban pleasure-ground!—the proper companions for these trees would be towering saurians to rub their scaly flanks against them or pluck the higher twigs and branches. I know nothing about the age of these trees— who does?—but what they look is far older than the Quaternary period, survivors rather of the Jurassic or Cretaceous, from a world before colour was or flowers or birds or mammals. They seem to have risen out of what Francis Thompson called "The Night of Forebeing," to be the first monstrous experiments in the shaping of life, heaving, straining in the throes of becoming, thrusting off the mass-weight of inertia.

And so, because we are incapable of picturing that phantasmal existence, they appear dream-like, a kind of Walt Disney world, except that they are less purely grotesque than his trees, which are in the Gothic tradition. They have might and they are a little frightening. Wondrous progeny of Giant Tellus, and under one I see an iron basket for litter and a few minutes' walk away is Teashop Road and Cafeteria Corner. The appalling triviality of our civilization hits you like a blow, coming out of Burnham Beeches. It becomes so nasty and trivial that it is much more frightening than the beeches. Did those trees sweat in growth and bulge in form that the travail of earth's beginnings should produce Slough at the end of it? The beeches seem to have been born in a world where man was not yet. They look, dying as most of them are, as though they must still be there when the poor forked radish has ceased troubling it.

II

THE WORMSLEY VALLEY (53, 54, 57, 58)

The rural graces of the south Chilterns are more intimate, tender and delicate than elsewhere within the interior of the range. It is not a country easy to describe for that very reason and, to the best of my knowledge, has, except for casual mention and brief pauses by the church at Ewelme (27) or the

50   To Lady Elizabeth Hoby

51   To Sir Philip and Sir Thomas Hoby, erected by Lady
Elizabeth

"Give me, O God! a husband like to Thomas,
Or else restore me to my husband Thomas"

50, 51   TWO HOBY MONUMENTS IN BISHAM CHURCH

GRAY'S BEECH, BURNHAM BEECHES

Norman tower of Fingest (87), been accorded much the same
regard as the maid who dwelt beside the springs of Dove.
There must be scores of high-flown tributes to Chenies and the
Chalfonts for a handful of words that commemorate Fawley,
Stonor and Little Bix Bottom. Just as well maybe, and I have
my doubts whether they would not stay the happier in their
retirement even from sympathy. But this seclusion is so well
guarded by their lack of ostentatious charms that I am fortified
in the venture not to describe nor even to praise them, but to
recapture in memory something of the fragrance they bestowed
on me.

For the purposes merely of this chapter what I have called
"The South" may be taken in three segments, the northerly one
between the Oxford-Marlow and the Watlington-Turville roads
(the latter only a chalk ribbon); the centre between this road and
the Henley-Oxford arterial one and the southern section on the
other side of it. In the top-layer there is only one hamlet—
Ibstone—the rest is an intricate labyrinth of winding criss-cross
valleys ramparted by wooded downs. A handful of farms has
been scattered over the more open ground and "Houses" there
are but two, Ibstone and Wormsley. Though the London road
is part of its shore-line, it is as purely agricultural and nun-like
a piece of country as any in England. There are only two or
three roads that penetrate it and only one of these, a private one,
is of any length. Even along the public one motors are rare,
since it leads only to the head of the Hambleden Valley, and off
this road, horses, carts and ploughs are the sole moving objects
but for the hare among the root-ridges, the coney in the border-
strip between wood and topped pasture and the wind in the trees.
The white fallows run up like a scale from the treble to the green
turfy slopes and they up to the darker and deeper greens of the
woody crests. Nothing but the jingle of harness or the crunch
of the cart-wheels on the flinty white road or the evening muster-
call of the partridges or the silver shaft of the wren's challenge
from the litter of branches at the corner of a wood splinter the
summer quietude. Only here and there does the eye detect a
scratch from the mad world without upon the still inviolate
surface of this fragment of traditional England. It is as perfect,
as harmonious and self-contained in its way as Jane Austen is
in hers, and under the sunlight it is like hers a diminutive world
of crystal clarity whose rhythm, order and stability even modern
economics have been able to impoverish indeed but not yet to
dislocate. That will come when taxation has finally driven the
Fanes out of Wormsley House, but until they go this little Finland

is safe from the urban monster. The soil is none too indulgent to the share, though the pastures are of that old turf that ripes the sweetest mutton. The farming (by Mr. Stevens in particular) is good, balanced and zealous and therefore not too mechanized. Has the scene ever been different from end to end of the chain of human husbandry? It seems that it could not have been and that the Wormsley Valley is an eternal moment like a drop of dew but changed by some magician into a moonstone.

From its southern end the insinuating valley road travels on a shelf or terrace of the batter to the downland wall and all the way slides along the slope of a string of opening and closing valleys, faithful to their turns and vagaries. Only once does it dive into a beech-wood where the humus overhangs the little white cliffs of the chalk on either side, and the roots of the beeches, clothed in red moss like mittens, clutch the thin soil in long talons like the pictures of demons in old engravings. Trails of pendulous ivy explore for a hold. The rubbly road jumps out of the wood like a spring out of a hillside, and in the taking Chiltern fashion curves upon its course with oats and wheat on one side of it and the beechen edge on the other, while in August the oat-stooks succeed the gilded ranks of the wheat. The valley that does everything by halves and nothing long flows out into a broad bowl painted with the white of fallow, gaudy splashes of mustard, the brownish russet of the shocked oats and the warm gold of the wheat below the green rim of the turf embossed with woodland above it. Here on certain days the cloudscape peers over the ridge like an Alps dwarfing the little valley to a nutshell. Even the slopes as high as the tree-line catch the infection of variety within a microcosm, since open down alternates with dense woodland like a succession of plates in a camera.

In this lonely and yet always companionable region *Campanula glomerata*, the clustered purple bell-flower of gardens, grows wild with the succory and scabious, distinguished from the ivy-leaved bell-flower by the more intense colour—purplish-blue—of the flower-heads and their congregation at the extremity of the stem. No setting could be richer than the curving shelf whereon it is most abundant. No fewer than ten species of orchis and helleborine survive in this valley, but what they are and where they are I shall not say. I dare to say, however, that the summer snowflake (*Leucojum*), exceedingly rare as a wild flower, grows not a hundred miles away, and from my garden (which has a spring border of this proper Perdita's flower) I can look over the plain to the hills where it does grow wild. The wild snowdrop is abundant in the woods and one of the very rarest beauties in England—*Daphne mezereum*—has a very small colony hereabouts, while the spurge laurel is common. Sheep, too, occur on the tilted pastures like balls of thistledown at the distant end of the valley, and I fancy that there are fewer sheep on the Chilterns and more commons to graze them than in any other area of downland between Beachy Head, Weymouth and the Wash. Another twist in the valley or valley-complex and a hanging wood, tinted to a green shade even in the high noon of the year, engulfs the road at the foot of the slope. The wood falls down upon the white road like a breaking green wave over a ship in the trough of the sea. Leaving Wormsley House at the bottom of a deep dell on the right, it uprears, emerges from the torrent of leaves and climbs out into the arable land at the backdoor of Beacon Hill. The sudden view of the vast plain from the edge of the road between Christmas Common and the London road (15, 32, 33) is like coming out of a warm closet lined with books and filled with Staffordshire figurines and English water-colours and Windsor chairs into a huge and empty hall. The little rowans by the wayside are a valediction.

III

THE HAMBLEDEN VALLEY

The Wormsley Valley is a moment of poignant intimacy and in terms of country what the duet between Jessica and Lorenzo at Belmont is in terms of moonlight. As delicate if not quite so monastic is the chain of valleys to the south that culminate in the Hambleden Valley. A road to the east descends into it from the high ground for a journey of just short of six miles. It passes Ibstone and its Common, which is becoming the spit of dozens of other hamlets and commons away to the north-east because it is becoming residential. The fate of Ibstone is the sadder from two very fine things about it. The first is that one of the cottages contains one of the best interior bread-ovens in the South of England. The other is that the natives, what are left of them, are extremely tenacious about their grazing rights on the Common *which still belongs to them*. The contours of the long lean parallel ridges nosing their way south towards Nettlebed and Turville and bearing heavy woodland on their backs, are well defined from the Common. Farther south, they spread out like the spokes of a wheel or the fingers of an outstretched hand and the observa-

tories of the Vicar of Fingest come into sight down the valley.
Like beehives they are, and on the eastern side the Old Windmill
on the crest gathers the fluted lines of the radiating valleys to it
as though they were its green sails. Its black conical top, white
weatherboarded middle and black brick base make it the very
lighthouse of these solitary miles.

As the road passes between Fingest and Turville, the multiplicity of these valleys increases (54) and at one point seven come
into sight at once, winding in and out of one another like a
giant's maze. Sheep like cloudlets stipple the inclines; the white
chalk fallows are like tablecloths laid for some pastoral feast-day,
and the aspect of the whole seems the discovery of some Arcadia
floated down the stream of time, but silent, expectant and un-
tenanted. The fall is steep into the Hambleden Valley that
introduces a softer, fatter, more lowland country with the hills
sinking into lower retaining walls. A full-bodied promontory
bends over the village like a branch over a stream, and this is the
gatepost between the uplands and the widening water-meadows.
The transition to Thames-side is exquisitely managed, since the
meadows, pushing back the hills, go down to the fine Mill,
the Lock, the lasher, the islands, the Thames and a new kind of
well-fleshed country quite different from the Perdita-like grace of
the Turville valleys. It is not surprising that the prosperous
Romanized Celtic landlords built a string of villas along the
delectable slopes between Turville, Fingest and Hambleden.

But Hambleden (55) is of the kin of Turville (56) to the
north rather than of Medmenham, its neighbour to the south-
east. The one is Chilterns with a dash of allaying Thames,
the other Thames-side with the plumed ridge nodding over it
as though to hold it back from yielding altogether to the
dubious sweets of that too tempting valley. Medmenham (49) is
rustical rather than rural, and the lazy white smoke curling up
from the flint cottage at the foot of the toy chalk cliff suggests
that the guardian is asleep. There is more timber-framing than
on the flinty hills, the trees are denser and the vegetation is
altogether more bowery. The whole village is indeed smothered
under a load of creepers like a woman in a fur coat, and the ivy
that mats the Abbey walls, hiding the building, seems at once a
cloak thrown over its seamy past in the days of the Dashwood
and a symbol of the lassitude and decay that follow upon high
and gamey living. I believe that Hell-Fire Francis himself planted
ivy over the studiously ruined cloisters, and now the whole
village is so bosomed in creepers that it looks more than a little
run to seed. It is a pleasure to get back to the honey-coloured,

53 SUMMER IN THE WORMSLEY VALLEY, NEAR TURVILLE

54   THE HILL-RIDGE GROUPING ROUND TURVILLE AND FINGEST, FROM SOUTH END

conical, sharply pointed ricks that stand between it and Hambleden and so between Thames-side and hillside.

Hambleden has a little open triangle that is all curves at its middle and a chestnut in it, roads that curl out into the hills, a rosy-bricked Elizabethan manor, waggons and tumbrils in black weatherboarded barns, fine local iron-work on the four turrets of the flint church-tower (55) on one side of the triangle, a string-course of timber across a cottage close by and another of brick on a cottage opposite it, a vine climbing the flint-wall of a third cottage in the "square," a Georgian rectory and a row of cottages with bow fronts and old roughcast parallel with the stream just round the corner. It thus looks very much more robust than Medmenham, though actually it is disposed along the valley in an easy-going layout in keeping with its position at the head of a kind of land estuary going down to the sybaritic Thames. But it remembers that it is also at the foot of the hills and bears the appearance—this "valley-on-a-slope" as the name means—of having had a good solid country tradition behind it.

This tradition is twofold, each deeply harmonious with the other. On the one hand, the slopes of Ridgewood and the meadows of the winterbourne are proper to many orchises, though musk, military and some others have gone. The valley is also the only area in the Chilterns where the redshank still breeds. On the other, both lace-making and straw-plait were full industries there in the early nineteenth century, while in 1640 the parish registers inscribed ten yeomen, a bargeman, a glover, a weaver, a bricklayer, a carpenter, a lath-shaver, a wharfinger, a miller, a "mayson," a smith, a wheelwright, a flour-maker, a hemp-dresser, a shoemaker and a joiner. Nothing could be more effective than that list to illustrate the utter poverty of village life in the twentieth century nor the extent of the robbery by urbanized finance of the national chest. For the wealth of a nation was and always must be contained in this list and all other riches are, as we are beginning to find out to our bitter cost, illusory. The list also actualizes the bond that is deeply felt between the network of interwoven valleys—all on a miniature scale and like a design in Bucks Point Lace—and the toylike aspect of the villages. They translate the nature of the country into human terms and an inventory of the husbandly craftsmen or craftsmanly husbandmen who made Hambleden uncovers the fibres of that bond.

One of these yeomen was named Rockall (he was "buried in linen" in 1704) and there is a Rockall, a chair-bodger, living and plying his craft not three miles away to this hour. This Samuel

Rockall and my good friend (p. 60) perfectly illustrates in his person and in his work the intercommunion not merely between Man and Nature but between a purely local type of craftsman and the particular country at his threshold from which he draws his daily bread.

Turville, that bright berry of the southern Chilterns, is a hill-and-valley village, compact, domestic and yet prodigal in architectural variety, so that it might be considered to fuse the cosiness of the valleys with the freedom of the hills. The real interpretation, I think, is that it remains a traditional Chiltern village, not as yet attacked by the flying spores of urban settlement. Its close cluster round the squat and massive tower of the church unconsciously reflects, that is to say, the compression and near neighbourhood of ridge, spur, headland and valley which mark the landscape of the Chilterns, while the diversity of the cottage fronts (56) are a human expression, equally instinctive, of the multiform shapes that every corner of its intricate system reveals. Timber, flint and brick are shuffled together in all kinds of ingenious variations within a very small space. If the average Chiltern cottage be examined, it will be found not only that these materials are interchanged one with another in different combinations, but that the brick-work, when used as a framing, is formed into a variety of geometrical patterns. In one cottage I know (near Stonor) flint and *single* bricks form the walls. The addition of triangular dormers of whitewash, of white arched windows in the eighteenth-century neo-Gothic style and moulded chimney-stacks either in the centre of the roof as at the Bull and Butcher or semi-detached on a shouldered base, makes a yet livelier impression. Only the russet tiling remains consistent, but the pitch and angles of the roofs are full of change. To crown the whole, the Old Bakehouse has a vine up its wall that produces abundance of sweet grapes.

Except for its pleasant inn, the church tower and an enchanting cottage of rosy brick within a timber frame resting on a flint base, crowned with twin gables and flanked by a brick chimney of possibly Tudor date, Fingest on the other side of Turville Hill to the east, is much more nondescript. Also it is going at the edges like a leaf in October by means of the callous uncouth building on its outskirts. Let Fingest go since it is doomed, if only we can keep Turville. On the hills round Turville, pigs are frequent in the pastures, there are ricks on staddle-stones and the acrid pungent smoke of the autumn bonfires in the stubble carries the spirit into the deeper satisfactions of the old life, the true and timeless life of husbandry. Glow-worms are Nature's

55 THE OUTSKIRTS OF HAMBLEDEN VILLAGE

56 COTTAGES BY THE GREEN, TURVILLE

57   THE UPPER PART OF WORMSLEY VALLEY, FROM NORTH END

58   WINTER ON THE DOWNS NEAR TURVILLE

candles here; an occasional corncrake finds sanctuary and the goatsucker that Gilbert White cleared of the charge of sucking goats still nests, if less abundantly than of old, on the high ground of the Commons. On a spur of the Ibstone ridge an old recondi- tioned farmstead, Hell Corner Farm (60) expansive in shippons and bartons and commanding a generous view of the opposite slopes, suggests a fullness of bygone husbandry which is a thing of the past. The name had probably something to do with "St. Francis of Wycombe," but it is to be taken in the sense of Blake's *Marriage of Heaven and Hell* wherein hell has all the best tunes. A magnificent pear-tree grows in the gardens—the Old Town Pear—which reminds me of the pear-trees at Dymock, of the daffodils in the Severn Vale. It is probable that the barbarians will not pull down the saddlebacked, flint, Norman church tower (though you never know) of Fingest. A curious thing about it is that the crowning gables are of sixteenth or seventeenth century. It is thus a striking example of a new turn in the native passion for organizing brick with flint and flint with brick, and of its antiquity.

The very devious road up north from Medmenham to Frieth runs through the eastern limits of the authentic country of the south. It is very secluded, like that to the west of it, but the high ridge, climbing steeply, broadens into a semi-plateau, and this up as far as Woodend and Chisbridge Cross gives amplitude and strength of line to the sweeps of high woodland all about. Below Mousells Wood, west of Frieth, Blackstonia is abundant on the chalky slopes with scabious and marjoram, turned almost black in autumn. I fancy that the thin pauper look of the chalk soil where the elegant yellow-wort grows in such profusion marks the relapse of former arable which destroyed the old turf. As you travel, you become nebulously aware that something is missing and in the end you formulate what it is. The intimacy of the Wormsley and Hambleden Valleys is wearing thin and all at once you are at Frieth.

There is no doubt about Frieth being a boundary post. The fatal gift of beauty—the poets have always regarded it as in- separable from tragedy, and Frieth just comes into the area of infection from Wycombe to the east. There is one thing worth seeing in the upclimbing street and that is the topiary work of the yew in front of the Yew-Tree Shop of Emma Keep. The old houses have had a final "e" stuck on to them in reconditioning, and an amazing "modern" house, all grinning windows, is the *bonne-bouche* of a tempting-looking lane. Yet from the Brickmakers' Arms, a significant title. Moorend Common is visible on the opposite ridge, a place where snipe once nested by the willows, a place once famous for its nightingales, a place where the chair-makers were once in force, a place where smocks were the latest to be worn. Cut off west down the valley to Fingest and on the slope above the Chequers Inn with its admirable sign it is seen that the invasion is creeping out farther west from Frieth and Wycombe, eating up the true country as it goes, inexorably reducing its area. Yet the battle still hangs in suspense: all about is the real thing, set within its frame of woods and pastures. Even a Dutch barn appears less offensive than usual because at least it serves a purpose and is not sentimental like the Frieth houses. Frieth is frippery, for its new-comers bear no more relation to the country than a field labourer in smock and corduroys would have to Bond Street.

You leave Frieth for the pleasant woods and fields to the west of it. But you see no natives, the hay is uncut, the builder's poster stands in front of the farm-gate. The sight of the Old Windmill on the crest beyond the narrow valley of Fingest looks like a port in the storm. But that is an optical delusion: the port is silted up; the mesh of interlacing valleys east of Frieth awaits its doom with the smile of the Christian martyrs in Rome, and the metal standards of the Council notices, "Footpath" (in the best lavatory style), seem the pickets of the conquerors. In the middle of the fourteenth century Bishop Henry de Burghersh stole a portion of the village common land at Fingest. His ghost walked in consequence and he beset the canons at Lincoln with the importunacy of his remorse until restitution was made, the crime was undone and the spectre was at peace. But ghosts walk no longer: the dead are only too glad to be quit of the world and the living know not what they do.

IV

STONOR PARK (61, 63)

Feeling this chill wind at my back from the east, I judge it time to shift my quarters farther west and Stonor Park is a good jumping-off place for the rich experience of the complex interior that lies due south of the Wormsley Valley. Stonor lies at the heart of it and from its pastoral height the eye can enjoy the unique privilege of searching out all points of the compass without any disturbance of the harmonies. There are two entrances to the manor in which (the report has come down)

59 BIX BOTTOM FARM

60 THE OLD PEAR-TREE HELL CORNER FARM, IBSTONE

61   STONOR HOUSE AND PARK, WITH A HERD OF BROWSING DEER

Campion the Jesuit took refuge, a manor which is the eye of the park just below the thatch of the northern woods. One to the east is wooded, the other to the west open rolling parkland. There is no need for hesitation. The eastern woods are bordered with nut trees and sweet chestnuts, but are frowning within, and the path leads down through sombre aisles to a flank of the ridge massed with willow-herb. Below, the valley opens out, richly indented with woody spurs, to where Stonor House, screened by gloomy rhododendrons, is secluded from the world (61).

From the west, it steps boldly out of its leafy cloak to command the whole valley and the beechen legions marshalled in a wide semicircle upon the crests of its cupping earth-walls. Though books cock their heads admiringly on one side when they speak of Hughenden Park, that dreary pleasance, nothing in print exists about Stonor Park, though a more perfect setting for the house and a nobler house for the setting could not be. The virtue of a park as a constituent of landscape is that it should be intermediate between cultivated land or gardens and incult nature, a kind of self-governing protectorate wherein a nice judgment in leaving alone (as Capability Brown forgot) is practised. Stonor Park fulfils these requirements as few parks ever do. It is an undulating sheepwalk broadcasted with single or groups of trees and so a true semi-domestic variant to the wild and woody steeps that encompass it on three sides. The trees are diversified as they should be; elms, chestnuts, sycamores, crab prevent the autocracy of the dominant beech and the eye takes in the strata of a cedar's rigid planes from the green path above it. Mokes share the flowing expanse with the deer, and a foreign oak is decked with the sacred mistletoe.

But of all the trees of Stonor I love best the crab that spreads its boughs near the western lodge. There are of crabs three varieties, the yellow-green, the streaked and the red which is the rarest in the south and of chief excellence in the making of jelly. The Stonor crab is so loaded with the first of these, cheek by cheek, that if Blake could see a vision of angels in a tree at Peckham Rye, this gifted crab might well be the perch and shrine of Pomona, the gentle patroness of fruits. It is a galaxy of them. From the highest ground the eye identifies nothing along the sweep of that great amphitheatre, though memory knows the direction of every hamlet, wood or farm, one by one. There is nothing to be seen but the crescent of the woods, lofted upon their rampart. Parts of the manor are earlier, but its long low front to-day is later seventeenth century, warm red brick with a projecting gabled porch in the centre and little gabled dormers, Chiltern style, in a row along the roof. The chapel to one side has a bell-turret and the short wings at either end are punctuated with battlemented turrets, probably eighteenth-century Gothic with round-headed white-framed latticed windows (as at Turville) of the same date. The beading at the eaves is one of the innumerable lost arts of England as it is to-day. This ancestral house of the Camoys lies in a trough of the swell of the Park and just above it the woodland throws out a pair of depressed wings like those of a partridge skimming the hedge-top. The site is far more beautiful thus than had the manor been elevated on a rise. Few of the great houses look their best in prominence: pride becomes arrogance and dominance assertion. Stonor withdraws from the world and rules by beauty alone.

From the east, the only road to Stonor Park, which I have chosen as the core of this southern country, like the central boss of a lierne-vaulted roof, is by a lane through Gussetts Wood at right angles to the Hambleden-Fingest road. Gussetts Wood is beech but it has this curiosity that a gap has been cloven through it, and this has become waste land populated by birch saplings so densely that they block out distance. This broad belt reveals the beech-wood in a new aspect, the light mole-colour or fawn of the slender trunks against a tenebrous interior. At the zenith of summer, the Chiltern beech-woods represent that thickening of the light that precedes the dusk on account of the canopy of foliage that partly excludes and partly splinters and diffuses the rays of the sun. This, together with the lateral spread of the roots on the shallow soil of the plateau, accounts for the absence of the shrub and ground-plant layers, which is by no means true of beech-wood on deeper soils, where the root-run is vertical. Between Gussetts and the Stonor Woods stood, when I last saw it in August 1939, a many-acred field of wheat and barley, excellent in quality, and in the very centre of it, so that the bearded ail of the barley brushed against the posts, was placed a monster notice-board—Building Land for Sale. This is the serpent in this particular demi-Eden, this the writing on the wall that spells its doom.

From the south up to Stonor a road forks from the Henley Fair Mile past the Deer Park of Lower Assendon and the saw-mills of Middle Assendon. This and the road up the Hambleden Valley to the east are the only straightish roads over the whole area covered by this chapter. The queer thing about it is that, though the most direct route from Henley to Watlington and beyond, it has been let alone. Has the Council been deaf to the trumpets of progress? Why is it not pouring out the ratepayers' money and paving that road with gold? The wayfarer in incredulous gratitude murmurs, "let sleeping dogs lie," since road and valley as they are make parts of a single composition. The slopes of the valley, narrow but not pinched, flow down from east and west to their natural place of meeting—the road—and their gradients are of just the right inclination to display their Jacob's coat of grey fallow, green down, golden wheat, barley of silvery fawn and white cloudlets of sheep (for there are a few sheep in this favoured valley), as though they were laid out as beautiful cloths for the special appraisement of the traveller along the road. The woods too vary in position, now furring the crests and then dipping to the road, at one place pent up and at another thinning out into a backscreen for the open fields.

At the heel of this valley, the road passes the village of Stonor, still genuine. It possesses a fine collection of porched, flint and weatherboarded barns and some good houses, some with projecting whitened bricks used ornamentally, while another has a double string-course of brick running across the flint walls. When the Chilterns were occupied by their native folk and every workman had scope to exercise his inborn taste and craftsmanly faculty, you can imagine them giving play to their fancies as to what variations to introduce into the arrangement of the materials at their disposal—flint, brick and timber. Not the least part of the felicity of this valley are the bridle path notices. For some inexplicable reason (possibly the happening of the county boundary), gone are the vandal-urban "Public Footpath" signs, and the discretion of their forerunners, plain white fingerposts and planks, seems like works of art in comparison with the vulgarity, a stage below even seaside lodging-house taste, of the metal standards.

V

THE HEART OF THE CHILTERNS

But it is from the west that I best love to approach the crabtree in Stonor Park, and the more circuitous the way the better. The country is not only as secluded as any in England but packs into a small space those highly distinctive characters of the Chilterns that entitle them to specific rank among the generic recognition-marks common to the chalk uplands of England. The pleasantest of the two most direct routes from Howe Hill or Cookley Green—with its lime avenue and surround of conifer, sycamore and chestnut behind which the cottages are modestly retired (Stadhampton in the Oxon plain is a larger example of a similar structure)—is by way of Russell's Water and Maidensgrove, nowadays both euphemisms. The road is open and margined with turf in front of tall bracken, while the eye takes in most of Greenfield Wood over Pishill Common to the north. Red tile-roofs pierce the close vegetation of coppice edges, and the road after the wide expanse of common plunges steeply down into a dark wood splashed with sun and out in front of the great curving amphitheatre of Stonor Park, with the complex of spurs, folds and bosses round Pishill to the left, and on the right-hand the long diminishing lines of the valley that lead down to the Fair Mile.

Maidensgrove is perhaps the most remote hamlet in all the Chilterns and stands on the crest of the eastern wall of Bix Bottom. The steep slope, called the Scrubs (62, 64), is one of the reminders that the Chilterns were once a wild impenetrable forest-land. The Scrubs are a toy wilderness of pigmy oak and bracken on clay-with-flints, honeycombed with little turfen paths winding snake-wise down the hillside. The golden time to be among these oaks, dwarfed by the winds as though topped by a billhook, is on a misty day of November when every tree is a pale copper, and you can look over their heads down into the Bix Valley filled with a plum-coloured haze like grape-bloom, yet not dense enough to obscure its junction with the Stonor Valley to the north. A contrast as intoxicating can be seen on the slope of Chinnor Hill when the purple bloom of the juniper berries and of the fallows below is seen against the red gold of the invading beeches. The loss of this way to Stonor is its brevity, its advantage that it enables the questing eye to grasp as a balanced whole two of the main structural principles of Chiltern uplands—open commons and plateau scrub as a foreground, a bottom flanked by thick woodland falling down the dip-slopes from the ridge-face like a spate of water over a Thames weir.

But the south-easterly road from outside Cookley Green to Little Bix Bottom is in point of quality the nearest thing to that through the Wormsley Valley that exists throughout the Chilterns. There are lengths out of the Fingest Valley that are its equal, but none of a similar continuity. Where ploughs are set out opposite an ironmonger's workshop at Park Corner is the right beginning to a true road, being flint-made still and so white, for the limestone as pale gold is the natural road-colour for the Cotswolds. Between high banks and backward-sloping downs the road descends past Devil's Hill through open woodland of

62 THE MIXED WOODLANDS OF THE BIX BOTTOM TRACK FROM
MAIDENSGROVE SCRUBS

63 ACROSS STONOR PARK

64 THE GAMEKEEPER'S COTTAGE ON THE BIX BOTTOM TRACK, WITH THE WOODS RISING TO NETTLEBED, FROM MAIDENSGROVE SCRUBS

the mixed kind that shows the chalk to be no longer the surface soil (68). Scrub alternates with a thin woodland of oak, ash, beech, sycamore, yew, crab, holly, birch, hornbeam and cherry, that true Chiltern tree, which in their turn foster a "subclimatic" underwood of thorn, elder, hazel, buckthorn and whitebeam, that true Chiltern bush. So diverse is the scene (62) that there is still room for large colonies of bracken and willow-herb to fill the empty spaces (and these grow to a height that might shelter any outlaw from twentieth-century urbanism, except that none escape it. After a wet summer the bracken would tickle his ears and the willow-herb brush his hair). In late summer the drifting down of the willow-herb crosses the little flinty sandy road like migratory drifts of small mealy-winged moths, diffusing a heady scent which really comes from the bracken. In autumn, it is ghostly in seed like tufts of swans-down or sheep's wool. At midsummer it floats over the hillside in a cloud of lavender. Nut-trees are very abundant, producing neither cobs nor filberts but the rounder wood-nut, and in the clearings the delicate little centaury contrasts with the languid fronds of the bracken and the lusty rosebay throwing its high pyramidal spires. The only thing against this wild piece of land is that it is a pheasant preserve, as a walk up one of the turfy paths will soon advertise in the shape of a gamekeeper's larder. Not all the arguments advanced in favour of preserving pheasants as a means of preserving the country will persuade me that it is not an ignoble cult and the gibbet its barbarous technique of sacrifice.

I am inclined to think that this woodland is a fragment of the original Chiltern mixed forest dominated by oak and so established previously to the colonization of the interior open chalk by the beech, following upon the desertion of the heights by the Romano-Celtic villagers. This rather than beech forest was what the barrow-builders of Whiteleaf encountered. The fat loam is extremely rich in humus and from it protrude large flints like boulders in a shallow mountain stream. It is noticeable that only the oaks are of wide girth and spread, while nearly all the other trees, though old, have leaped up on long attenuated poles with hardly more than twigs for lateral branches (68). I have never before seen wild cherry growing so tall and branchless. This would seem to indicate a fairly recent clearance of close-growing timber, and this in its turn points to natural oak-forest rather than semi-natural coppice-with-standard forest. Whether I am on a false or a true scent, there is no doubt at all that this most interesting piece of woodland is rapidly degenerating, and one of the principal reasons is without doubt—the gamekeeper's gibbet. By destroying the natural hunters of mice and voles, pheasant-preserving is directly responsible for their multiplication and their excessive increase arrests the self-regeneration of forest lands by destroying all the fruits, acorns and mast. A merciless game-preserve will thus in the end always defeat its own purpose.

Once, amid the shrilling of the grasshoppers, three shires came pounding along the road, the shaft-horse jingling his harness against the flies, all of them chequered by the sunlight, the beams playing over their thewed flanks and haunches, captured in the nets covering their stalwart withers and flickering down their ear-caps. They dragged a big timber-waggon behind them, and only the absence of latten-bells upon the hames and rubber for iron-tired wheels prevented my being the spectator of a scene, complete in all its parts, from *The Woodlanders*.

The errant road bounds through the valley, responsive to its caprices of form and showing off the downs on either side in new shapes and positions at all the turns which, being numerous, give the impression that they are in perpetual motion. Passing now a splash of ragwort or St. John's wort or glittering holly, now through a tunnel of beeches or sun-filtered shades of oak, it pursues a lithe and free course in tune with every change in the hills. Steep hillsides bossed with scrub stride out to meet it (62, 64), retreat, reform, close round it and open until it emerges from the woody glades to run between wheat-lands and shoulders of open down, a rare sight among the Chilterns. Here within a curved bowl of land, chalk supersedes loam and the Great and Black Mulleins the willow-herb until the road comes within a few yards of the old ivy-ruined church of Bix Bottom, an object-lesson to those who think of ivy as "picturesque." As soon think of a stoat as picturesque in the act of sucking a rabbit's throat. The sentiment aroused by the ivy that has crumbled the little Norman church like a python crushing the bones of its prey, like Germany crushing Poland and Russia Finland, is one of horror.

At Little Bix Bottom, where there is an admirable group of bartons, the road forks, one ribbon going south past Turnpike House, a flint-and-brick cottage as intimate as the countryside, to the old turnpike from Henley to Oxford, the other curving east to Middle Assendon Smithy, where it meets the north-and-south road to Stonor. At Middle Assendon there is another fine barn and a Georgian round-headed window in the middle gable of the three-gabled Rainbow Inn (66). Thence a connecting road turns north again to Fawley Bottom, leaving Fawley in its eyrie to the right (the name is usually a sign of Roman occupation) and fetches up at Gussetts Wood. This stretch is inferior, if at all, only to the Wormsley Valley. Farmhouses and barns are the only buildings—the difference between them is that the ones have more windows, the others more materials in their structure, being seldom less than four. When they are in good repair you may take it for granted that the land is still decently farmed. In other words, the Fawley present shows some signs of continuity with the Fawley past, and that is a heroic achievement, a noble resistance in the great war of the town upon the country. The roofs of russet tile are just what the walls of flint need to carry off their coldness, though brick and timber are as effective for the purpose. On the edge of the great plain some of the roofs of Stanton St. John are of the same terra-cotta red on walls of oolite limestone. This is quite as it should be, since the beautiful village is on the frontier-line of the clay and the limestone. All the same, red tiling is less perfectly married to stone than to the brick- or timber-framed flint walls of the Chilterns.

Mixed woodlands are generously scattered and the road curls past the edge of a wood with cornfields on the other side; then round two or three more corners woods and arable change over like partners in a dance. This is a mannerism highly characteristic of this miniature, changeable, delicate country, seldom grand but always endearing where it is untainted. Orchards still further diversify it, and oats are a frequent crop, a heartening sight in a land where the farmers according to the crazy economics of to-day buy their fodder crops from abroad instead of raising them themselves. It is hardly necessary to add that neither rye nor flax, linseed, excellent crops for milking cows and fattening calves and at their best on the light shallow soils of the Middle Chalk, are grown as they used to be. There are even hairpin bends, and pieces of the Berkshire hills across the Thames valley appear and disappear over the beech-hedges. The cows are sometimes Jersey herds, and the field-gates sometimes built with the bark left on the spars and braces. If it is not great country like the Cotswolds and the Sussex Downs, it is less sophisticated than they are rapidly becoming or have become, and so traditional and so honest. It is still its own self, a lovable minor verse but without a flaw in the lyrical cadence.

Fawley Court, once plundered by both parties in the Civil War and yet more fatally by its subsequent restorers, lies down by Henley Reach. But church and hamlet perch on a windy mount reached by a lane or rather tunnel roofed by foliage, walled with hedges and pillared with yews, from one of those

H

grassy bottoms that are quintessential Chiltern. Fawley has a
few snug little whitewashed houses warmly tiled, but its curiosity
is their contrast with the gigantic tombs in the churchyard, itself
ponderously towered. One, set up in 1707 as a family vault of
the Freeman family of Fawley Court, is a round tower of freestone blocks with a domed top and a straddled plinth as though
the weight were too heavy. The other, that of the Mackenzies
who succeeded them at the Court, is square with a pediment, and
more presentable because it is less ostentatious. This pair of
tombs revives the Neolithic tradition of the family long barrow,
broken in the Bronze Age: they were the portentous burial
chambers of the local Fawley chieftains. It is queer to think that
their originals go back to a time long preceding the use of the
wild Chilterns as a refuge to the Romano-Celtic Christians from
the Saxon Pagans and to outlaws from the domestic chaos of
Stephen and Maud, the Wars of the Roses, the Tudor Enclosures,
the Puritan persecution and other causes that produced vagabondage and free-booting, that in their turn produced the stewardship
of the Chiltern Hundreds—Stoke, Desborough and Burnham.

The greater part of the approach to Stonor from the north is
contained in the parish of Turville the minute, so that it is like a
filbert inside a walnut shell. I am unable to separate this dear
retired niche of the hills from its human associations. North
End (69) and South End, Turville Heath and Summer Heath
for me are hieroglyphics of Samuel Rockall, the chair-leg
bodger (p. 60). I have never known a craftsman—and I have
known a good few members of this moribund genus — who
could be more fittingly described as the flower and excellence
in human terms of his particular natural environment. It is not
only that he is dependent for his livelihood upon the beech-
woods at his door, felling the trees himself, carrying the timber
himself, which is sawn, stacked, chopped on the chopping-block,
riven on the splitting-block, dressed on the draw-shave horse,
shortened on the sawing-horse and turned on the wheel-lathe
by himself alone. It is something more than that. He can hardly
be called the sylvan deity of his heaths and woods, and yet he is
the intermediary between this microcosm of Nature and the
traditional needs of humanity. He is the child of Nature, the
genius of his place, but in a special sense which is mediæval, not
Greek, and yet catches something of the Greek idea, just as
things made for man's daily use by the practice of inherited
craftsmanship are inevitably and yet incidentally beautiful. Beauty
is the by-product, and in the same way the poetry and romance of
Samuel Rockall are the by-product of his trade, his happy bird-

65   THE SOLITARY GAMEKEEPER'S COTTAGE BELOW
MAIDENSGROVE SCRUBS

66   THE RAINBOW INN, MIDDLE ASSENDON

67   THE OLD GOATKEEPER IN THE FAIR MILE, HENLEY

68   SPRING IN THE BIRCH COPPICES OF THE BIX BOTTOM TRACK

like spirit and his lifelong devotion to his craft, his family, his countryside and his independence. Thoreau was a stranger to his woods beside Samuel's intimacy with his.

His cottage of flint and his "hovel" of timber are the only buildings but one on Summer Heath, and both have become an integral part of the bracken and old thorns and beechen girdle of the heath. The avenue leading into it fits in as perfectly. It was planted after the Armada but is more Gothic-looking than Elizabethan with the tree-bases just like the base-mouldings to Early English pier-clusters and composed of lime (both the Common and the less familiar Small-Leaved—*Tilia parvifolia*), sycamore, beech and wych-elm. The trees are very rich in design with their taloned roots, striated barks and ogee-shaped branches dipping almost to the ground. The cottage is one with all these but Rockall himself is more intimately, yes, and spiritually so. A kind of blessedness emanates from the man as it does from the woods that surround his home when the wild snowdrop shakes its bells of annunciation there under the February beeches.

Since I have written much of him in previous books, I shall say no more of him here except in respect of my last two visits to him, both since the War, the second Great War, I mean. The first time, he was still as busy as ever and presented me with a spoke-shave whose owners he traced back for more than a century—indeed I have quite a large collection of the Rockall tools reaching well back into the early nineteenth century. This reminded him of his grandfather who was both hurdler and bodger. His wife was tart and contumacious and one day in a difference threatened to drown herself in the pond at Northend, where the little white house stands above the pond like Beachy Head above the southern sea (69). Off she went and he, snatching up his fiddle, followed singing to the music, "My wife is going to drown herself." Seeing the impression made by her decision upon him, she turned back and came home again and he changed the wording of his tune to, "My wife's come back and bethought herself." On the second occasion, Samuel (after presenting me with one of his earliest draw-shaves) was found ball-turning a barber's pole of ash that before the War had been turned by machinery. Thus, the barber's pole had returned to its traditional home, and it is more than possible that the shafts in the angles of the tower at Fairford are painted with a spiral pattern in two colours in deliberate imitation of the barber's pole. I feared that Samuel would be one of the victims, innumerable as the leaves of autumn, of an age to which craftsmanship is an antiquarian curiosity. I feared that he would lose

SAMUEL ROCKALL AND SON

the thirty shillings a week that progress pays him. Apart from the chain of wars that are the note of our century and constantly have threatened his livelihood, there is only one other bodger in the parish of Turville where in 1900 there were thirty. But no, he was still working.

VI

THE WOOD-BODGER (13)

The main interest of the southerly section of the tripartite South—the Wormsley Valley for the head, Turville, Fingest, Fawley and Hambleden for the body and the heavily wooded region south of Nettlebed for the tail—centres in the villages and rural environment of Stoke Row and Checkendon. Stoke Row is a deceit and a paradox. To travel down the long street on its windy ridge is to pick up a totally erroneous impression of it. Apart from the minor curiosity of the mosque-like dome erected over the very deep well of the village by some Maharajah or Nabob, you appear to be nowhere which is what Suburbia makes of somewhere. The touch of it annihilates identity in place just as the theory and practice of the State in modern Europe annihilates individuality in person. But Stoke Row as a native home has not been expunged from the face of the Chilterns like scores of their less fortunate ones; the real thing, driven out of the main street, has taken refuge down the by-lanes, behind the fine cherry-orchards of the neighbourhood, in odd corners and niches where no casual explorer would dream of looking for it.

Yet more surprisingly, Stoke Row is a beehive of local craftsmen. Behind the Cherry Tree Inn, for instance, set well back from the contaminating street, lurks one of the very few surviving bodgers who uses the pole-lathe and, over seventy as he is, still (or did so before the War) turns out three gross of chair-legs every week, not, oddly enough, for the Wycombe factories but for Scottish chair-makers. Stoke Row is like a centipede for the number of flinty old lanes that sheer off at right angles to the main body, and one of these sneaks off south through Basset Wood in the neighbourhood of luxuriant heath, commons, glades and woodlands where the funguses under the beeches grow like tables in a fairy-story. At Heath End, a couple of the bodgers of Stoke Row (they live opposite the Hope Inn) have their camp in the woods. But their wood-turning is already an anachronism and to-day they make tent-pegs only (13). One of them, grey-haired but full of vigour, told me that he had long abandoned his traditional craft. The Wycombe machines had knocked him out. "If I was to make the chair-legs I used to forty years ago and offer a Windsor chair to a young married couple, they'd think I was mad." He himself had made such a chair for his own wedding that time ago and "it's as sound as a bell to-day." But now the people whose taste has been vitiated by the Industrial-cum-Machine Age want "something fancy," and that is not work, he implied, for an honest man. He used to make legs for rush-bottomed as well as Windsor chairs out of

THE POLE LATHE: MR. SAUNDERS OF CHECKENDON

cherry-wood as well as beech. Cherry-wood chairs took a fine grain if well rubbed with sandpaper which was fitted into the wheel-lathe that turned them. His lot was a standing example of the inherent hostility of our economic system to the craftsman, of mass-production to home-made work, of the machine to the inherited aptitudes of hand and eye and, I would add, of frivolity to beauty.

Another of these lanes—this time on the northern side—drops off the ridge of Stoke Row down through the cherry orchards to the Crooked Billet (71). It is a snug white-washed brick pub with green shutters and russet roof standing on a base of black flints. Nasturtium runs wild up the hedge opposite and a

69 THE POND, NORTH END, ABOVE TURVILLE

70 FINGEST AND THE WAY TOWARDS LANE END,
FROM TURVILLE HILL

white cow steps twice daily past a black weatherboarded barn. Within, there is a grand open fireplace with ingle seat, bread oven and a good fireback, and this is the home of Mr. Silas W. Saunders, the pole-lathe turner. All day he works in the woods which wash over the spurs, cols and ridges of this area in seamless billows of foliage, and it is as hard to locate him as though he were an outlaw found sanctuary among the piers of the ecclesiastical beeches. But a landmark of the flowing woods and steep sequestered lanes is a great tree, a beech, 160 feet high when measured thirty years ago, soaring up from the tiny spires of *Epipactis latifolia* in the wood. The bole, scarred with initials up to six feet, shoots straight up like a rocket from a mossy base without projecting roots and then proliferates into seven or more branches set out with the symmetry of a rose. The absence of horizontal roots visible on the surface or just beneath it is a conclusive indication that the chalk is overlaid by loams or clays. What do not these woodlands owe to the bodger who has worked for so many generations under their shade? The reason why they make such well-proportioned growth and spread such generous crowns is because of his knowledgeable thinnings, and his extinction will be followed by their immediate deterioration.

"The Tree" is a direction post for miles round and in the dell below is Bottom Farm with a pair of staddle-stone erections and good sharp-angled stacks. The farm sits between a pair of great woody horns of tapering land, one of which is Devil's Church Wood and the other where Mr. Saunders had, when I was questing him, his temporary "pitch." When his "thinnings" are done, he moves on to another quarter, always alone now that the days when his father employed six men are as remote as an Antipodes of time. At the tips of the canopied horns the land opens out into free rolling downs without a building in sight and here in his green bower the wood-bodger was camped.

A russet carpet of shavings dotted about with trestles and neat stacks of chair-legs is the approach to this rural altar, roofed and walled with corrugated iron. Was it not something better than the shrine of some furry wood-god to find a man in the midst of Nature who drew the material of his calling from Nature, laboured with the tools of Nature and followed the simple laws of Nature in the lap of her peace? No traditional craft—unless it be quarrying oolite roof-slats—reveals such a variety of processes from A to Z, each one of which is in so close a communication with Nature. After felling and carting from November to March when the sap is down, the natural product is always split and then chopped on separate blocks but never against the grain of the wood. The final treatment of all, that of the turning after the shaving on the draw-shave horse, the testing of the lengths by the gauge and the sawing to 18 inches for Windsor legs, is actually as primitive as the initial axe-work. That is because the wood-bodger—and Mr. Saunders has been one of them from the age of eleven to fifty-eight—turns the leg on the pole-lathe. The slender tapering pole protrudes through a square opening in the wall of the "hovel" over the lathe. It is always of larch or beech (if the sapling is straight enough), not ash or maple as has been incorrectly stated. If larch, it must have been rooted in the chalk and not in clay where it grows "a yard a year" and so, like ash, would be too flexible. The supports of the lathe itself are rough uprights or "trees," one at each end cut down to a height suitable for the two parallel planks (the "rest") that are the bed of the lathe and take the poppet heads. The points of both centres with their "thumbscrews" to tighten them are fixed (on Rockall's wheel-lathe one is movable) and the leg is adjusted between them. The cord fastened to the end of the sapling overhead is given a single turn round one end of the leg, wetted and attached to the treadle beneath, a triangle with point behind the worker and crosspiece on which the foot works, the chisel being applied on the downward stroke when the leg is revolving inwards.

Thus the adaptation to Nature is as complete in the ultimate stage along the scale of treatment as it was when the axe struck the first note in a tune to which the woodland setting of the "hovel," the blocks on the floor, the axes and saws hanging on the wall, the knee-deep shavings under the lathe and the very clothes of the master-man all harmoniously contribute. The short-handled steel-edged chopping axe is made specially for the craft, and that of Mr. Saunders's father is now in my museum. It would not be possible in any period of human history or prehistory to point to a human labour in more perfect accord with Nature nor one so utterly contrary to the theories and practices of automatism in a mechanized society. Silas Saunders was more lonely than in being alone with only the beech-trees for company. He was as lonely as a solitary rock in an ocean of void and turbulent waters. Rock is the word, since for any craft to survive, much more one so rooted in Nature, among conditions that are the antithesis of its particular ethos, is something like a miracle of tenacity. The crafts do not change; they are exterminated by pressure from without, but they neither progress nor decay from within, because each craft represents a series of creative acts within a traditional mould. The crafts solve the problem of human stability and to a large extent of social economics because

creative activity by master-hands continues through the centuries
detached from the disintegrating factors of over-production,
financial manipulation and speculation, mechanized servitude
and a landless proletariat, until these and allied elements prove
too much for them. Then they perish but never because there is
no further need for them. Fundamental human needs always have
been the reason for their existence and the community is always
in consequence the poorer for their death. Every country craft,
that is to say, has a more or less remote ancestry.

How long chair-leg turning has been a Chiltern trade is an
irrelevant issue. The question to ask is, how long has wood-
turning with the pole-lathe been a human industry? After looking
up the scant information available, I gather that the pole-lathe
represents a development from the Bow Drill as shown in Bulleid
and Grey's book upon the crafts of the Glastonbury Lake
Village. The Celtic bowl-turners of 50 B.C. were the true ancestors
of Silas W. Saunders, and it is probable that his genealogical
table goes still further back into the unchronicled past. The discs
in Kimmeridge coal-money and shale bracelets were certainly
made off some type of pole-lathe and they were in use during the
Late Bronze Age of 1000 B.C.

But the day of Silas Saunders is nearly done, and there is none
to take his place. Nowadays he makes only plain "church" and
Windsor legs and spars, but the demand even for them is rapidly
falling off both from the extension of machinery in the trade and
increased dependence on cheap and inferior foreign woods. The
master-men of to-day are all of ripe years and apprenticeship,
indispensable to the continuity of the crafts—it takes years to
learn bodging—has ceased since 1911. In the old days the hovels
used to be thatched with fine twigs and the bodgers, according to
the right balances of former husbandry, were mowers, reapers
and thatchers in the summer and chair-makers or chair-leg
turners in the winter and spring. Now all the bodgers I know
work at bodging alone against an attenuated demand.

In the wood near Bottom Farm I was in at the death. I could
be a witness to the changeless rhythms of country crafts and
experience their organic unity with the Icknield Way, the Celtic
camps on the hills and the dim recesses of the beech-woods just
previous to the extinction of one of the very oldest and most
primitive. Talking to that patient, soft-voiced, mild-spoken man
with the spectacles and listening to his tale of resignation within
the core of Nature's undying life, I could know the true, the
timeless England at the moment of its last sigh. Yet the in-
destructible reality seemed to be in the tonal harmony between

I

the skirr of the chisel and the murmuration of the wind in the
high beechen tops rather than in the forces of the raging world
where neither one nor the other is heard. In his *Journal d'une
Révolution* (1937), M. Guéhenno wrote, "Je crois en une mission
de France. . . . Si la révolution est le mouvement qui détermine
dans une société le besoin de dignité personnelle, la révolution est
une vieille, très vieille chose en France." Such a revolution has
been already achieved in the Gothic idea of the master-craftsman.

VII

The Wood-Village

There is much indigenous woodland in the southernmost part
of the South Chilterns, and this environment is proper to the
pole-lathe, as wood-bodging is to the days when workmanship
counted and men were happy in the satisfaction of it. The tradition
that the Romano-Celts held out more stubbornly in the southern
region than elsewhere is likely to be connected with the greater
extent there, not of the beech-woods whose advance was probably
later, but of mixed forest. A large area is of this type with much
yew and holly but less juniper than farther north. The usual
notice-boards that these woods are for sale as building sites meet
the traveller at every turn. Between Stoke Row, Highmore and
Nettlebed, the country is more like what Surrey used to be than
it is in other regions, due no doubt to the deposits of gravel and
Reading Beds over the chalk. Woods, heaths and commons are
close neighbours; lime and birch are prominent and the sandy
open tracks are girdled with pines. Since he is less conscious than
he would be in Surrey that a stockbroker's residence may lurk
down every sandy lane, he sees the heaths as less sophisticated,
less like urban recreation grounds than in Surrey. Nettlebed, too,
is less victimized by the main road running through it and past
the derelict rounded cone in red brick of the pottery-kiln than,
by analogy with other villages so misfortuned, it should be.

We have thought of Carl Moritz and the frequently recurring
blacksmith's epitaph he noted (p. 4). It is pleasant to think that
this young German pastor-writer, who incurred every kind of
unpleasantness by touring England on foot, found at Nettlebed an
agreeable oasis from the snubs and black looks which formed his
constant portion. Here he was received with tolerable civility and
comfort at The Bull, in the building which is much as it was then,
though the beam sign has gone. Here he joined glad-heartedly in

71 THE "CROOKED BILLET," NEAR STOKE ROW

72 BARN INTERIOR, CRABTREE FARM, MIDDLE ASSENDON (*v.* FIG. 14)

73   Interior looking East   74 A Norman Capital of the South Door

75   The Exterior from the South-East

CHECKENDON CHURCH

the Sunday morning service, of which he has left so graphic and moving a picture. But it was the bright friendly atmosphere of the little place that brought solace and cheer to his bruised, lonely spirit, so that he "seemed indeed to be enchanted," and it was only at the fourth attempt he was able to wrench himself free from his "favourite Nettlebed," and tramp onwards to Oxford on his way to Derbyshire.

Checkendon (Oxon) on the summit of one of the ridges at the south-western corner of the interior still holds on to the present as an authentic village, though some of its fingers have been knocked off. Like those of so many other hill-top villages in the Chilterns, the houses are ranged about a little triangular green with the church at one corner. There is a strong personal style about the genuine village homes of the hills: you would know them anywhere. They are very compact with low roofs, nearly always red-tiled and very seldom thatched; they often have neat tiled triangular dormers with latticed windows and the timber framing is rarely obtrusive. They are not at all cramped within, are well-balanced in structure and fertile, as I have said, in the varied combinations of brick with flint. One cottage at Checkendon is of flint, brick and timber with plaster as a filling: possibly it is wattle-and-daub. Another has a plinth of both brick and flint; in another the base is as high as the upper storey. The attached chimney with its broad shoulders crops up again and this mannerism reminds me of the rather heavier stacks in the Vale of Tewkesbury and the Worcestershire plain. Tudor tops to the shafts are by no means uncommon.

Unhappily, Checkendon has obviously been discovered by week-enders and a rash of bogus has broken out: here and on the way to Rotherfield Greys houses have been built or more probably reconditioned which ape the reality without concealing the imposture.

With the exception, of course, of that of Ewelme and of Fingest Tower, Checkendon Church (73–75) is far and away the best in the South. But it is a cripple to what it was before the nineteenth-century ecclesiologists, who fully shared the bad taste diffused by the Industrial Revolution among the whole population, removed the box pews and the floor tiling, ejected the canopied pulpit, inserted glass that turns the stomach to look at and committed other atrocities. It is Norman with a rounded apse and arabesque capitals to the piers of the arches (74) and the porch has a holy-water stoup as at Bledlow. But what most strikes the eye, if it can stay blind to an altar-cloth that would disgrace the rites of a Solomon Islander and floor tiling suitable

for the feet of a negro dance-band, are the spacing and proportions
of the body of the church, which is crowded with sumptuous
monuments. Most effective is the double Norman arching into
the choir and again into the apse (73), and when the apse was
squared and the chancel became one with the choir, it was a
severe loss in grandeur. Both these arches together with the
tympanum and jambs of the south doorway are richly decorated
in the intricate, fantastical, late Norman style. The free use of
billet and dog-tooth, the roll-moulding of the chancel-arch, the
corbel heads, the bones of the open timber roof, the brasses—
none of this rich ornament compromises the lofty monumental
serenity of this interior and almost without knowing it the eyes
are guided to one of the chief distinctions of it. These are the
murals that go right round the east end of the rounded apse
(73). High above the altar Christ in Majesty is seated on a
throne with Peter and Paul under crocketed canopies flanking
the central figure. Curving round the base of the throne are sprays
of clover, exquisite in design, while the rest of the Apostles are
ranged on either side of Peter and Paul, very tall, proudly haloed,
each with one hand uplifted in praise. I only know one set of
murals to equal this noble group and that is in the minute church
of Stowell, not far from Bibury, unless it is also the set in the
little old disused church of Kempley near Dymock, in Gloucester-
shire. There is nothing in the least crude nor angular about them:
the disposition, robing, grouping and expressions of the figures
are all good, but that is not the reason why they are exceptional.
It is because the master-craftsman has conveyed the impression
of holiness, an emotion antiquated by progress. The figures have
been fetched out of the wall, so to speak, but not indiscreetly
nor with the prettifying effect of the retouching of the fourteenth-
century murals at Horley near Banbury.

Below a Renaissance monument of 1673 in the choir (a mask
puts out its tongue in it—a salutary gesture when the pomp and
vanity of many Renaissance monuments is considered) is an unusual and lovely brass of a soul clasping its hands and supported
by two angels on either side with outspread wings as though but
just alighted. There is radiance in this brass and the detail of the
wings is masterly. I should have liked to have brought Cobbett
to see this church. Checkendon is a hamlet and yet here is a large
church capable of seating a congregation living in a village four
times as large. The preponderance of hamlets over villages in the
Chilterns indicates an early and primitive type of settlement, but
Checkendon was evidently a large village at one time that has
degenerated into a hamlet. Cobbett frequently dilated upon the

big churches in the little villages and he knew what that meant
—depopulation and the eating up of country by town. All his
forebodings and prognostications have been more than fulfilled
to-day when the nemesis of that exploitation is seen to be the more-
than-possibility of famine. It is to be hoped that his indignant
ghost does not walk.

From the Four Horseshoes it is possible to travel some true
Chiltern country, the way these heavy-bearded hills used to look
when the works of man were in harmony with them, when Man
and Nature made *one whole*. Then, when you find it, suddenly the
country comes alive: it is no longer dead in the present but alive
in the past.

This, with many exceptions, is true of the way to Rotherfield
Peppard and Rotherfield Greys east from Checkendon towards
Henley. It is a country of forested uplands, sloping meadows,
little commons, turfy ways winding into the shadows of the trees,
deep lanes of beech hedging and deep bottoms with embossed
walls. It is a better country in winter than in summer because
the woods are less ghostly then and the complex structure of
wood, slope and ridge is seen in its proper modelling. Beech-
woods in summer tend to cloud over the shape of things. This
country is distinct from that of the heaths of Highmore to the
north of it and from the warm gracious rusticity of the Wormsley
and Turville Valleys. Cornfields are much rarer and the woodlands form great squares and circles round the tilted meadows.
The two Rotherfields are both built round greens, one, Peppard,
large enough to throw a veil of distance over the kinds of houses
that surround it. Things to notice are the transitional Norman
font at Rotherfield Greys, the surprising frequency of the elm
and the hornbeam that usually dislikes high ground, the sporadic
appearance of thatch and the not ineffective resistance the
beechen legions are putting up against aggression from Reading
that is only five or six miles away.

The difference in respect of urban invasion between the interior
of the South Chilterns and that of the East and North is so great
that I took some trouble to find out the reason why. That the
South is not quite so accessible from the Wen and its satellites is
true, but an indifferent argument. The kernel of the South from
the point of view of rural integrity, not to mention intrinsic
beauty, is the Wormsley and Turville Valleys. Both are within
easy reach of High Wycombe by car and of the London road by
Shanks's pony. How comes it then that they remain legitimate
English country and have not been bastardized by the rape of
that country? The reason is not because they have not been

attacked but because they have been defended. Some time ago plans were submitted to the Wycombe R.D.C. for 62 houses to be built upon 87 acres of land between the Turville Valley road and the Northend-Turville Heath road. The attempt of the land-owners of the region, including Mr. Fane of Wormsley House, the saviour of the Wormsley Valley, to nip this pretty little scheme of urban rapacity in the bud failed, I gather, from lack of support, whereupon the Wycombe R.D.C. Joint Town Planning Committee passed a resolution that no house should be built on less than 10 acres of land. Thus for the time being the Turville region is still *virgo intacta*, snatched, indeed, out of the very hands of the ravisher and safe at least for the period of the war. But its release is only temporary, its immunity precarious, since the cannibals who get their loot out of preying on their own native land are always active, always ready to seize any occasion which will deliver this precious thing, this piece of unsullied England, into their grasp. In the meantime, let every patriot who happens to read this page, every Englishman with a spark of sensibility and any sense of values above the aim of feathering his own nest, offer up a silent word of gratitude to the Wycombe R.D.C. for defending his country against the barbarians.

There are people who express surprise at the nature of the world in which we live to-day, who feel that the German violation of Poland and the Low Countries and the Russian of Finland are an inexplicable repudiation of European civilization. They are nothing of the kind; they but carry to their logical extremity the principles of economic expediency set in full motion by the Industrial Revolution and written as visibly if not in red ink upon our own native soil as upon the bloody fields of Europe. If that accursed spirit is not exorcized in every country and not merely in the most offending, not the Chilterns only but Europe itself are doomed.

76   THE EIGHTEENTH-CENTURY DIRECTION-PILLAR, WEST WYCOMBE,
       WITH THE CHURCH AND MAUSOLEUM BEHIND

78   Church Lane, with the fifteenth-century Church Loft at bottom

77   The George and Dragon Inn

V

THE WYCOMBE ORBIT

I

THE WYCOMBE VALLEY

IN many places, particularly in the north and east, the Chilterns are, as I have said, a minor lyrical poetry, fragile, delicate, feminine, full of graces rather than grandeur, a kind of spunglass beauty. But there are certain areas which rise to the dignity and inspiration of major poetry and one of these without doubt is the eastward flow of the parallel ridges to their convergence at the head of the noble valley of the Wycombes. High on the central and open ridge is littered the bastard village of Bledlow Ridge. The effect is quite different from the sentimentalizing and vulgarizing of the tenderer beauties of the hills by modern building, because the fine chiselling of the valleys, the diversities of form in the clean strong lines of the flanking ridges, clothed in heavy woodland, the symmetry of the composition cannot be undone by the insect discharges of twentieth-century man. The neglected fields, the brutal notice-boards of building sites, the hash of irrelevant houses merely leave a stain of nastiness that an honest broom could sweep away. At the pitch of the great moment when the parallel ridges from Lodge Hill and Venus Wood draw to a centre and sink into the valley-head buttressed by Church Hill, and when the eye experiences a Shakespearian climax, it is confronted by a row of the meanest possible houses, worthy of High Wycombe itself. But even this blotch, placed by monkey cunning just where the eye comes to rest, is unable to rob the hills of their special moment. Rather it demonstrates the insignificance of twentieth-century civilization in relation to the changeless values of Nature.

How magnificent is the staging of that moment! The very yews increase their density as a means of punctuating the roll of the ridges dipping down in long curves into this node and core of the uplands system. I do not know how many valleys meet here, because the four major ones—spreading out starfish-wise towards High Wycombe, Princes Risborough, Chinnor and Radnage—tuck subsidiary ones between them, no more than toy combes. The way to gather them up like reins into the fist is to climb the "Hill," and the massive carving of the scene is enhanced by the grouping of the beech-wood crests, the dominance of Church Hill in site and elevation and the smooth fall of the surrounding ridges to the bend of the little River Wye. It is a landscape design as no man could ever conceive it, and yet the deliberation of the ranges in meeting at this one point appears as purposeful as the convergence of long trains of pilgrims towards a celebrated shrine.

Man is always best when he follows Nature, and if he could never create such a scene, he could take perceptive advantage of it, and did. The shrine was once at this very spot, a wishing well; there are cultivation terraces on Church Hill and three camps of undiscovered dates dressed Keep, Castle and Church Hills in lines of the proper downland curves. A Roman villa was built near the site of West Wycombe Manor on the opposite slope, while the Church Loft (1417) on its flint and brick plinth with a seventeenth-century clock faces the London road. Once a mediæval hostelry with cells for monks, it has carved upon its corner-post the matrix of a crucifix, removed by Hampden's Puritan army, and a kneeling block of the local sandstone from Walter's Ash below it. There was no beggar, chapman, pilgrim, minstrel, university student nor pack-horse traveller along the highway between Canterbury and Walsingham, London and Oxford, who did not stop there to kneel and pray. Sir Francis Dashwood made the new road in 1752 and set up the Pedestal Sign-Post (76) whose sandstone blocks have been removed by the Council. But long before that droves of Welsh sheep, goats and ponies on their way to the East Anglian fairs paused to drink at the stream close by, while the drovers bent the knee at the wayside shrine and drank from the holy well.

Thus the convergence of peoples responded to the confluence of the hills, and the great valley of High Wycombe is like a broad estuary, wider than most of the Chiltern valleys, to match what seems an act of symbolic deference on its behalf by the crested hills. From the summit of Church Hill, the eye can discern the full contours of that most shapely valley, the receding hills curved back as the Red Sea was split and retracted for the host of Israel. The ribbon of the River Wye, that was the instrument for carving so deep-bosomed a gap, and rises in the Long Meadow of West Wycombe, now steals along the southern flank with a group of bartons as natural to the earth as a group of trees, beside it. When High Wycombe was a Georgian town and straw-plait and lace-making were industries within it deeply compatible with the neighbouring countryside; when chair-making was the real thing, not a commercial organization for faking the antique and supplying machine-made chairs to people who can no longer recognize the difference between living and mechanical work, the works of man were worthy of so benignant and yet proud a setting. Cobbett called the pre-industrial Wycombe "a very fine and clean market-town; the people all looking extremely well; the girls somewhat larger-featured and larger-boned than in Sussex and not so fresh-coloured and bright-eyed," and praised the region for the earliness of its wheat. If he had seen it from the top of the "Hill," would he not have exclaimed and slapped his thigh with joy as he did when he looked from a high place down the valley of the Salisbury Avon? What the observer sees now from this Darien is the scoop of the valley used as a gigantic rubbish-dump. It is a vast dustbin of houses. If we wrote our names over the surface of a Michael Angelo statue and scribbled rude drawings upon it, what a fuss and fluttering! That is exactly what has been done with a valley carved by a greater than Michael Angelo.

Church Hill is as grand as any in a loving memory of many a one I know in downland, and its crown is bare, though a great wood that once bore the name of the lost village of Haveringdown on the saddle clothes its north-western shoulder. Its flanks are stippled and streaked with yew, many of them, the hoariest, cut down, others mutilated, but a sprinkling of veterans survives that can hold the heaviest shower off a man. The groves known as Little and Great Pen are still standing, though shorn of their archaic splendour with their sanctity. Quite apart from the earth-work of customary Iron Age type round the Church of St. Lawrence and the Celtic place-name for the valley, this is an indication that the "Hill," like Swyncombe Downs, was a Celtic *locus consecratus*, while the village below was founded early in the eighth century. Harebell, scabious, pink yarrow and cow-parsley crown its head with garlands in summer; the pyramidal, musk and bird's nest orchises graced the wood up to recent years and the great and black mulleins and the bloody crane's bill (perhaps the finest of the geraniums) still survive if very sparsely along the meadows and lanes. Like the art of its Celtic settlers, probably the first men who ever set foot on it, it expresses itself in company with all true chalk mounts in the curve. When I turn my head from the Wye Valley and pick out a group of farm buildings clustered above the tanned stubbles to the north, I can see much the same as the villagers of lost Haveringdown saw twelve centuries ago. Hawfinches nest on the Hill and the red-backed shrike has his summer residence there, and these were about their business above the flowers when it was a sacred site of Paganism and when the thirteenth-century church was built in the centre of the earthwork to record the fact.

II

THE PAGAN CHURCH ON THE HILL

The odd, the incredible fact is that in the eighteenth century it returned to Paganism, thus reversing the universal rule of our land, that Christian churches by the wise decision of Pope Gregory were founded upon the sites of Pagan shrines. The "Hill" has had extraordinary permutations indeed in the history of English religions, and in that respect is unique in England. First, Iron Age Celtic or bastard Greek, then Christian and still Hellenized, then Oriental-Hellenic and lastly Christian again in our own day, if anything in the twentieth century can be called Christian. It is, I think, possible to infer, not from documents but simply from observation of the church itself (80–82), what in rough outline the religion was which by the fiat of the Chancellor of the Exchequer, the Lord Despenser, dispossessed Christianity in it. Every guide-book without exception is earnest to smooth out the frowns of tradition and reinstate him as a very pretty if rather too dashing a Dashwood. The *Highways and Byways* regards him as "eccentric" and points to the chief of his vagaries in building a church on a hill, which he did not do, since there was one there already. Why it should be eccentric to build a church on a hill, the properest and most natural place on the earth for a church, is not explained. Nor do these books explain why they are at pains to whiten the sepulchre of the Franciscan chief of the Hell Fire Club. I have sought the reason up and down in my mind and have come to the conclusion for want of evidence that it is due to our incorrigible passion for a lord and, still more so, for a lord with a great deal of money.

The tradition is, of course, that the "Franciscans," the "Twelve Apostles" who were more than half of them in the Cabinet and, most of them, died at an advanced age in a halo of respectability, practised devil-worship both at Medmenham Abbey and in the flint caves of the "Hill" (the stream within was called "The

79   THE VILLAGE STREET OF WEST WYCOMBE, LOOKING EAST

80　The Armchair Pulpit　　　　　81　The Font

82　The Exterior from the South-East

80–82　WEST WYCOMBE CHURCH

Styx"), possibly too in the Golden Ball that looks so very like
a solar symbol on the top of the church tower (82), the
upper storey of which this Dashwood added to the fourteenth-
century tower of "clunch" blocks quarried from the caves.
John Wilkes, one of the twelve, at any rate made it so un-
comfortable for the rest of the infernal devotees that the Club
was disbanded. It seems dubious to me that a nobleman who ruled
the country both in and out of London should waste many years
of a long life in the warped-childish perversities of invoking the
Christian Satan, and it is a good working hypothesis, when the
"nave" of the church is entered, that he did nothing of the sort.
It is true that "St. Francis's" tutor overdosed him with religion
in his tender youth and that the Brotherhood wore the robes of
the Franciscan Order. But the evidence for "devil-worship"
rests only on the famous or infamous story of the baboon
released during a "service" at the Abbey, and Johnstone's *exposé*
in "Chrysal or the Adventures of a Guinea" suggests that the
rites were mainly those of vulgar venery and their priestesses
trollops from the London stews.

It is only by catching the atmosphere of the "nave," by
examining its furniture and linking these impressions and infer-
ences with more recondite evidence that something more
intellectual than mere lechery and less crude and sadistic and
puerile than mere Satanism may be gathered from the freaks of
"St. Francis." Half-way up this pseudo-nave is the font (81), a
tripod supporting a slender shaft with a snake curled round it in
pursuit of doves clustered round the bowl—a lively piece of
Italian baroque. The acolytes only used the nave which was
transformed in 1763 into a highly ornate drawing-room with
stout fluted pilasters exfoliating into Corinthian capitals, swags
of flowers, cornices of flowers and fruits, birds and foliage,
marble floor and plaster ceiling of rich mosaic. But on the ceiling
of the discarded choir or chancel, where there is some Grinling
Gibbons carving, is another dove surrounded by solar rays which
even a Chiltern guide-book could hardly mistake for the semblance
of the Holy Spirit. Doves, snake, flowers and fruits, magnificent
Chippendale arm-chairs set on chests of drawers (80) (there
was no pulpit) for the celebrants, what do they suggest but an
eighteenth-century revival among a thoroughly Pagan aristocracy
of the old Oriental worship of Kybele, Rhea and Aphrodite?
Snakes and doves were the inseparable symbols of the archaic
snake-goddesses of the Mediterranean and of Aphrodite of
Paphos who was descended from them. Such symbols, such
revivals were properly in tune with the statuary on the southern

slope across the valley and with the orgiastic meetings at Medmenham. My theory is a mere feeler but it happens to square very
appositely with a stray sentence in A. H. Plaisted's *The Manor
and Parish Records of Medmenham* (1925): "Here (in the chapter-
room) the Eleusinian mysteries of the pagan Franciscans were
performed with great secrecy and libations were poured forth
in great pomp to the Bona Dea." The same writer speaks of
West Wycombe Church being rebuilt "in the Grecian gusto,"
as an "atonement for his excesses." That is absurd: say rather
as a semi-philosophical development of the Medmenham
hedonism.

There was some sense and much piquancy from the point
of view of a corrupt dilettante with a great estate in Walpole's
"rosy anchorites" inventing their own debased version of an
archaic cult (with which Despencer's rather perverse learning
and Italian journeys and sympathies could have acquainted him)
within the very church devoted to the religion that had destroyed
its Pagan aftermath. Black masses and nasty mumbo-jumbo of
the Aleister Crowley type were small beer in comparison with
such a half-serious, half-ironic restoration. The conversion of a
Christian church into a Cyprian temple could only have been
possible to a landed aristocracy with autocratic powers, with the
parsons in its pocket and limitless resources as spoils of the
Enclosures. It is entertaining to think that the High Priest may
have consciously fostered the dark legend of his ritual demonism
because he knew that it would serve as a screen for a neo-
classicism that even the eighteenth century, semi-indulgent to
Satanic loyalties that were still a left-handed Christianity, would
never have tolerated. It is still more so to note the royal arms
over the chancel arch of the Temple of Love.

The extreme laxity of eighteenth-century morals combined
with the extreme power of its rulers and the extreme sycophancy
of its clerics towards that power has presented posterity with the
astonishing spectacle of an elegantly appointed Italian drawing-
room for the meetings of devout Cyprians in the nave of a
Christian church set high on the crown of a hill among the
Chiltern forests, once a beacon for pilgrims passing below and
kneeling at the Church Loft crucifix. Granted that this Dionysiac
rather than demoniac did carry the classical prepossessions of his
age too far and that he desecrated the ancient church on its
sacred mount, yet I fancy there is more to be said for his goddess
than for our contemporary god, the brassy philistine Plutus
whose lust has ravished the fair Valley of the Wye. This Plutus is
worse even than the Pluto that Sir Francis is presumed to have

summoned from the great depths. And as we have seen on the continent of Europe, the demonism of a modern mechanized society is far worse than either the Despencer Tartarus or the Despencer Paphos. The story of West Wycombe Church and Lord Despencer is not just an "eccentric" incident in the social history of the Chilterns. It is a spot-light, baleful and lurid, in the surrender of the Christian church to a secular government based upon wealth and material power alone. That is my excuse for examining this incident at some length.

A little distance away through the trees is the hexagonal Mausoleum (76) whence the souls of the departed cultists (the heart of the sinister poetaster, Paul Whitehead, chief agent of the Franciscan voluptuaries, once reposed there) might wing their way to the Isle of Cythera. It is as silly a building as ever I saw in my life. A few urns with grinning faces on them and a pretentious monument to Duchess Sarah remain. No recording observer has noted the round-headed arches. There are over forty of them, all of flint as the whole building is, and some of them loftier and wider than the Norman doorways to parochial churches. These niches and portals—the taller supported with horizontal dressed blocks of Portland Stone—are of exceptionally good workmanship and it is curious to reflect how very rare in England is the flint doorway. What futility that this nobleman with his talent, erudition, taste and riches should have frittered them all away on his antiquarian sensuality instead of doing for his neighbourhood something of what Coke of Norfolk, one of the very few rich men who knew the way through the needle's eye, did for Holkham and English agriculture!

III

THE TALE OF WEST WYCOMBE

The spectator of vanishing England may well wonder whether the village below this fantastic mount was worth the protective wing of the National Trust when it is a mere avenue of roaring streams of traffic in constant spate. The contrast between Sir Francis's elevated nave-drawing-room on top and the Church Loft below the hill is less acute than that between the village and the road that passes through it. The double row of joined houses seems only a façade, a painted backcloth, against the crude over-whelming tyranny of that road. None the less, the effort of detachment should be made. The village is not only a very beautiful one in its architecture (79), its outdoor signs and its wrought-iron brackets, but most instructive to the student of social changes. The structure of the little houses covers five centuries, from the fifteenth to the early nineteenth. Their fronts are very various in consequence. Grey flint makes a house-wall with cream-washed brick. The bow window and the Queen Anne railed outside steps come between overhanging upper storeys on moulded beams with the chief joists supported by brackets, the oriel window and gable-end. Wattle-and-daub between a thin timber framing is near neighbour to examples of the most fastidious eighteenth-century brickwork. Regency stucco shares the street with mullioned and transomed windows, casement windows, wide timbered archways and herringboned gables. Yet the general impression given by this double line of houses and by the numerous lanes, backs and miniature courtyards that with such fruitful variety lead out of them, is one of complete harmony. Imagine the hateful highway spirited off the scene and a unified village would present itself in which the walker would detect many variations not of kind but of degree.

This is extraordinary in view of the fact that, as we know, Renaissance, Queen Anne and Georgian architecture represents a very sharp break indeed with the native traditional style derived, as the Church Loft shows definitely enough, from the Gothic. The classical style of Inigo Jones and of his descendants in the fashion was a foreign importation departing far more radically from the Gothic in its aims and structural ideas than did the Gothic from the Romanesque. It brusquely interrupted the evolution of the native style. Why then do we fail to notice any discord between the earlier and the later houses of West Wycombe, and why do we see them as one and all members of one family? The answer is, I think, threefold. First, good workmanship has always a conciliatory influence, however diverse the technique and sources of inspiration: it is a unifying force. But the tenacity of the native style is a more powerful reason. Georgian and Renaissance country houses are not really country houses at all, they are urban houses built in the country. But the humbler type of house, cottage, shop and farmstead persisted in the old tradition, not with stiff-necked obduracy, but with an open-minded firmness that won concessions from the interloper.

This process of mutual goodwill is seen in being at West Wycombe. The mullioned windows of the George and Dragon Inn (77) are actually eighteenth century in date, while the Post Office of that period has wattle-and-daub in it of the sixteenth. The Plough Inn of 1743 has an open fireplace with an

83 VIEW OVER THE WYE VALLEY NEAR LOUDWATER,
HIGH WYCOMBE

84 HIGH WYCOMBE FROM THE SOUTH

85   THE MARKET-HALL, HIGH WYCOMBE

iron platform supported by brick standards in which there is a local fireholder called a "jinalin." One of the eighteenth-century houses through the archway of the Church Loft leading up the hillside to vanished Haveringdown (78) has an angel's head over the doorway which is pure Gothic, and mediæval hatching and moulding constantly occur on Georgian houses. A great many of the interiors of these gracious little houses belong to a much earlier date than do their fronts. In other words, it is not their date but their locality that counts. The *genius loci* was the spirit of continuity: division and experiment came from without but was constantly absorbed by the stability and durability of the rural tradition. That is why we do not really notice the difference in village architecture between one century and another. All were a product of the local craftsmanship; all in some inexplicable way that is not confined to the nature of their materials were subdued to the soil they live on. It was the Industrial Revolution that snapped the continuity, just as it represented a definite mutation in the social history, habits and purposes of the people. In West Wycombe the whole story can be read at a glance because the disrupting consequences of that Revolution are confined to the road. The overthrow of the spirit of place is seen in the road, not, by a stroke of luck, in the village which lines it.

IV

THE TWO WYCOMBES IN THE COUNTRY

The country within the orbit of the Wycombes, as I have roughly marked it out, occupies a middle region between the rural South and the more or less suburbanized country to the east and north. We should expect it, therefore, to offer a succession of the most violent and irreconcilable contrasts, and that is exactly what we do find. It is impossible to understand the Chilterns unless some attempt is made to define what is meant by such contrasts. It is an entirely superficial view which says—parts of the Chilterns are spoiled by modern building and parts are not: that is taking the animal's view of the world which is two-dimensional and leaving out the man's view which adds the dimension of thickness. It judges by outward appearance alone, but unless that appearance is regarded as expressive and symptomatic (as smiles or frowns on the human face are of states of mind), the significance of the country within the orbit of the Wycombes is missed.

This country witnesses by the conflict on its face the clash between two civilizations much more deeply divided than political parties are conventionally regarded to be. Local production, local subsistence which were the foundation of country life, however little they be so now, have nothing in common with modern economics, nothing at all, any more than the use of hand and brain have with machine-minding in a factory. They are opposites, just as what is home-made and home-grown are the opposite of what is imported from abroad. The peasant's lifelong contact with the earth means making something from within; the townsman's separation from it means getting something from without. These antitheses could be multiplied until the cows come home and all of them stress the central fact of conflict between one set of ideas, values, modes of life and another, a conflict whose issue is victory or defeat, not assimilation. These are facts; it is an expression of opinion that, since ugliness has been the standard of the dominant culture and beauty of the recessive, Nature has given moral judgment.

The conflict has been already decided; it is the country that has right and precedence over the town to stand as mourner over the graves of Polish and Bohemian liberties, the right of suffering and the precedence of dispossession. Round about the Wycombes, we come into touch with the conquerors and the conquered living side by side in actuality though utterly remote in spirit and we cannot grasp the essentials of this particular countryside without keeping this phenomenon in mind, one of the very strangest in our history. West Wycombe and High Wycombe are next door in the Valley of the Wye. So they are in the country north and south of the London road that travels through them both. And the contrasts between that village and that town are duplicated over and over again inside the periphery of the rural districts within easy reach of them.

The block of country south of the arterial road and northeast of Frieth and Fingest is a cluster of Ends and Commons whose characters call for no special comment except in so far as they are evocative. At Wheeler End, for instance, Abel Collins was the last survivor up to 1933 of the local Mummers who performed in the kitchens and inns. They used to rehearse in the kiln at Cadmore End Common. In the end he became the whole company, like Bottom taking all the parts. This saying has also been recorded of a Wheeler End bodger: "Cheer legs meead from split ood are alwiz better than them meead from sahn ood, because they goos wi' the greean while tothers ull breeak as soon as look at ye." Here too there was up to recent years a team of hand-ringers who

used to play the old ballad of the "Prickly Bush." Just as these
starveling recollections have been salvaged from the wreck of
peasant custom and ritual, so a few flint-cum-brick cottages, a
fine barn and the Brickmakers' Arms have escaped (like single
letters in the game of filling in the gaps to make words) to guide
retrospection back to the once unified hamlet encircling the
broad rough triangular common that still retains patches of
wildness.

Going south across the Stokenchurch-Marlow road, you come
to Moor End Common, once regionally celebrated for its sedgy
marl-ponds, willows, snipe and nightingales. The ponds still
exist and there are harebells on the Common, but the
"observables" are the extraordinary juxtaposition of bracken
with Suburbia, of the prettified with the desolate and austere,
like the Linton match in *Wuthering Heights*. As little good can
come out of the marriage of opposites at Moor End. At Lane
End between Moor and Wheeler Ends, there is a row of cottages
attached to the Chairmakers' Arms, where the flint is not only
framed with brick in the Chiltern idiom, but lozenges of brick
are set in a row above a string-course of the same material. These
cottages where the brickwork is geometrically interwoven into
the flint façade are dilapidated, broken-windowed and vacant.
They are the epitaph of Lane End. Cadmore End to the west
lacks even this memorial. Glimpses of the rolling, deep-bosomed
country of Ibstone still farther west are the sole reminder of what
it was.

V

A CLUSTER OF HAMLETS

The inner circle or rather crescent to the north, whose base
rests on the London road, tells the same story but with heightened
accents and in a more dramatic form. At the extreme north-
western point of what I have called the Wycombe orbit is Radnage,
which hardly any guide-book so much as mentions. Yet, it
preserves a self-contained serenity, an air of secluded order and
integrity which reveals the place as continuous (if only in appearance) with its past. By "place" I mean the church and a sprinkling
of discreet buildings at its foot. The church, whose walls are all
of flint, is small, twelfth century and Decorated, with a low squat
central tower not unlike that of Turville which is much bulkier.
Within, it has murals in the splays of the triple lancets at the
east end, consecration crosses, Saxon tub-font and an open

L

timber roof of the fifteenth century in the spandrels of whose curved braces arcades are carved. The present vicar has added furnishings of his own which give a unity to the interior, not of period (hardly a church in England has that), but beautifully expressing the slow harmonious tide of time, as seamless as the joins between the seasons.

But the rarer beauty of the church is in its position. The natural lineaments of the country there seem to have co-operated in raising a site and grouping a foreground of genius. The church stands on the crest of a small knoll thrust between two valleys converging into another at right angles to them and itself, edged by woodland, swinging off to its junction with yet another that meets it on a rounded corner. This succession of curves is in full view from the church-mound, and deepens not only the tranquillity of the actual scene but the sense of untroubled continuity from age to age. Directly below the mound is a small flint house with two cone-shapen yews as its portals. My last visit to Radnage Church was in time of war, my previous one six months before in time of peace, but the blessedness of the place exerted its dominion over both events, linking them to an assurance outside the flux of temporal things. Radnage lies in a cupboard of my mind as one of the most precious memories of the Chilterns I possess.

South of it lies "the City" whose spearhead is a tiny green lorded over by the Three Pigeons Inn; farther on, the place suddenly falls to pieces in a muddle of upland villas and things which are about as relevant to where they are as a child's scribblings on the page of a book. The long taut line of Bledlow Ridge makes a frontier to the north-east and the same pimplings can be seen along its crest. Take any hill-top village of traditional make as seen from a height at some distance away and its buildings will never look as though they were picnic litter strewn over it.

Bradenham, half the distance back to West Wycombe eastward from Radnage, is an oddity. Though spilling down a gentle slope right to the comely Red Lion on the edge of the Wycombe-Risborough road, it has by some miracle fended off the wolf-pack that surrounds it on all sides. How has it thus acquired the status of a sanctuary? The elder D'Israeli who lived in the manor behind its fine wrought-iron gates next the church (86) has been called the "prince of bookworms." Does that mean that he burrowed his way into the arcana of some cabalistic book which enabled him to lay a spell of *noli me tangere* as the magical warden of Bradenham? His ghost seems to have drawn a crescent south of Lacey Green, Speen, North Dean and Naphill Common

86 THE CHURCH AND MANOR HOUSE, BRADENHAM

87 FINGEST CHURCH TOWER FROM THE WEST

88   THE ENTRANCE PORTICO, WEST WYCOMBE HOUSE

89   THE "PEPPER-POT" LODGES AND AVENUE, HAMPDEN PARK

that leaves Bradenham intact in the middle, still *integer vitæ*. Hardly *vitæ* perhaps since they no longer cure the illustrious Bradenham hams there, though even a townsman in these days would wish with all his heart that they did. The church is built of flint rubble and is Early English, what is left of it, like Bledlow Church to the north-west. But the South Door is Saxon or early Norman, and the porch has curious arches supported on pillars with cushion capitals and enclosing a tympanum with lozenge decoration. It has, this minute church of nave, chancel and porch, a naïvely archaic air, and in the hamlet itself (a single line of cottages facing a sloping green) is a house with a castellated façade clapped on it—the Vicarage? Instead of feeling this to be a sham the impression accepts it as a gesture of unity with the church, so compact is the whole group of buildings. Thrift Cottage is one name that exorcizes all the "Bide a Wees" and "Mon Abris" and "Shalimars" and "Windy Ridges" that afflict the Chilterns traveller. Bradenham is a little kingdom resisting the predatory aggressor from without. An old-fashioned congregation, a tidy little museum-piece, they say. Yes, so left behind in the speed-mongering of progress that it no longer cures those hams our forefathers relished. There seems after all some advantage in "putting the clock back." Bradenham now leans against the hillside with nothing to do. It is a pity that big business prevents it from curing hams. We could do with them.

In Bradenham itself there is no violence of contrast to put a spoke in the wheel of continuity. The thud, the jar, the shock of interruption occurs along the chain of little communities strung out in an irregular arc between the Hampden area to the north and Bradenham in the south—Water End, Beacon's Bottom, Loosely Row, Lacey Green, Speen, Prestwood, Bryants Bottom, Walter's Ash and Naphill. The contrast is between them and Bradenham, since every settlement named has been either exterminated as a native gathering (Speen, for instance) or heavily invaded. The country is dimpled, scooped out and in certain parts I might say tunnelled into a network of valleys and bottoms, all on a miniature scale, running into one another and walled by a complex of hills until this land-turbulence is stilled on the eastward plateau of Prestwood and Great Kingshill. In places even the beech-woods are built up, and accordingly the thing to do is to detect relics of authentic Chilterns not so much from hamlet to hamlet as in the general body of them forced by this external pressure into an artificial uniformity. All along the belt Shakespeare's "And maiden honour rudely strumpeted" occurs and recurs to the mind.

A windmill varying in structure from others, for instance, occurs near Loosely Row, where there is a view most spacious. It reminds me of the Chiltern native peculiarity of a whole series of ingenious novelties and combinations within a pretty strict general formula of construction. This style recognizes its regional limitations, as all true art does, but is never hampered nor burdened by them. Below Speen, the prettified inn whose hostess is or was Ishbel Macdonald looks down upon as finely sculptured a glen, steep-sided and flowing in rich curves, as exists anywhere on the hills. From the summit I have looked down on the ploughman and his horses taking the furrows up and down the sharp incline as though Speen and not the rural tradition were the illusion. It contracts the heart that so douce and wayward a piece of country among these tangled valleys and dancing hills should have come under the harrow of the towns.

At Lacey Green there are two stretches of Grim's Dyke travelling nor'-nor'-east towards Great Hampden as a parish boundary and this is one more clue to its non-defensive purpose. Water End is now poxed with bungalows all over it, but at Beacon's Bottom close by, a slit in the uplands, a bodger—White—still turns his chair-legs and there are actually three others hidden away in odd corners north of Speen. The interesting thing about White's "hovel" is that it is thatched and there is more thatch in this region than any other known to me in the Chilterns. Here too the detached cottage chimney reaching its brick stack up from tiled shoulders and a base on the ground forms a conspicuous part of the sudden foreshortened landscapes. These with the thatch and colour-washed brick of the cottages indicate how individual each small pocket of this area once was, exercising its own choice, displaying its own preference within the boundaries of an instinctive deference to the law of materials. At Prestwood, again, the cultivated cherry tree still holds its own, as it does at Flackwell Heath between High Wycombe and Bourne End, at Stoke Row in the south, at Seer Green near Beaconsfield and between Chinnor Hill and Bledlow Great Wood. Between Prestwood and Great Kingshill is a chimney-stack built of flint, the only example I know.

In Bryants Bottom I once saw vividly how the tyranny works. This was once a local station of importance because here were extracted the blocks of white sandstone or puddingstone, similar to the silicate "Sarsen" stones of the Wiltshire Downs that were the making of the Avebury Avenue and Great Circle, not to mention the Trilithons of Stonehenge. These very hard blocks are sands of the Woolwich and Reading Beds, cemented by silica. They were probed by T-shaped skewers called "snipers," the difference between the flint and the sandstone being detected by scraping. The monoliths, some of them weighing 350 tons, were split *in situ* 64 feet down by means of mortice holes, hoop-iron, wedge and beetle, removed in pieces and cut into square "setts." Affections of the lungs were common and these were defeated by adapting the Wiltshire technique of "banker" tubs stood to windward of the stones, the air-current being regulated by wattled hurdles. Thus the sandstone dust was safely carried away, but now the industry itself is dust.

No sooner had this dingle fallen asleep at the foot of a curvilinear spur than the bungalows crept down upon it. They squatted just inside its portals as though afraid to commit them-selves to the loneliness of its depths and with as much congruity to the scene as the sheep that still graze on the down above the wire-fenced square enclosures would have if each were dressed in a bib, tucker and a pair of spectacles. They have taken the land, which is part arable, part sheepwalk, but never will they settle into it. At the other end of the Bottom gipsies were camping under the first trees of the wood that abuts on the fallows. Their painted caravan 'stood by and a brass-knobbed knife-grinder beside it as though the caravan had dropped its calf, while blue smoke from the camp-fire garlanded the glowing boughs of autumn. A more fantastic contrast between one end of Bryants Bottom and the other could hardly be conceived. The wanderers belonged, and for ever through the ages; the settlers would be foreigners until their gimcrackery fell to pieces.

The books do say something about Naphill Common—I never could make out why. They tell us that hollies and juniper, bracken and gorse, oak and scrubby beech grow there and that there are ponds and turfy paths. Granted, but this applies to many other commons, while the juniper, the most uncommon plant on the list, is of much finer growth elsewhere. My own impression is that Naphill Common looks like a particularly clever venture in landscape gardening; it is not so much wild as an attempt to look wild and so sophisticated. Maidensgrove Scrubs, Ibstone Common, Summer Heath by Turville make it look imitation because they are the real thing. What it may have looked like once is another matter but nowadays, in wandering over it, I feel as though somebody were looking at me from the bedroom window of one of the villas. All the region round the Common —except Bradenham—has been villafied and built over to such an extent that it has surrendered up its identity. It exists merely as the haggard ghost of itself.

Yet among these villas exists what is perhaps the greatest surprise in the Chilterns, and so a contrast indeed, a pearl, a wonder. No less a personage lives by Naphill Common than the very last of the Chiltern handicraft chair-makers—and him no book ever mentions. Edward Harold Goodchild has his proper flint cottage and next door to it his long low weatherboarded

DEAN'S CHAIR FACTORY, STOKENCHURCH

workshop with its sagging timbers propped up on poles. This lengthy interior is literally stuffed to the ceiling-beams with chair-parts—arms, legs, seats, splats, back-bows, skeletons—a glorious gallimaufry of everything to do with chairs, so that he and his assistant have barely room to work and move about. How the hens find a way in is a mystery. An armoury of tools—spoke-shaves, scrapers-in-stock, travishers, adzes, cleaning-up irons, mortising gouges and their fellows—hang from the walls

90　SNOW IN PENN WOODS

91　THE DESERTED TRACK TO VICAR'S HOLLOW, NEAR UPPER
VICAR'S FARM, BEACON HILL

92 BUNGALOWS AT BEACON'S BOTTOM

93 CONCRETE MODERNISM ON AMERSHAM HILL

94 COMMONWOOD HOUSE ON ITS COMMON, NEAR
CHIPPERFIELD, HERTFORDSHIRE

or litter the benches. Some have been designed by himself to
pick up the grain of the wood. Beside them hang designs in
paper and highly decorative banister-splats. I love a workshop
like this as well as any landscape: indeed, I find an affinity
between the one and the other. The smell of the shavings, the
feel of the timber in the making, the vast serviceable untidy
litter exhilarate me like wine. A workshop like this is a fundamental piece of reality, the dynamic link between Nature and
Man, and the spectacle of what Man can do when he is in tune
and in touch and in play with his mother-earth is an indescribable
refreshment and release from the hideous unreality of modern
life. Though the crafts are killed off one after another, there is a
sense of the undying about them, of a sweet permanence that has
solved the problem of adjusting means to ends, life to environment, beauty to need. The gigantic muddle of modernity, the
consequence of losing ends in means, is shamed before this
spectacle of creative order emergent from chaos. You know
that this is what really counts in life—this honest man making
handsome, solid, craftsmanly chairs out of the trees in his neighbourhood, oak, walnut, yew, beech, apple, pear, elm and
chestnut.

His tools are, of course, more elaborate than those of the
bodger, the number of the turning chisels is greater and, like
Samuel Rockall (who once made me a Windsor chair), he uses
the fly-wheel lathe. He steams his own backs from a tank in his
orchard. As among the chair-leg bodgers, every process from
A to Z passes through his own hands, and this is one reason why
the rhythms of craftsmanship bear so close a resemblance to
those of Nature and none to the routines of mechanical production. Mr. Goodchild has been a chair-maker for twenty-seven
years and of course his father was in it before him, though he
only made seats. The last time I was in his workshop I ordered
an arm-chair of yew-wood, chairs in this difficult wood being
some of his finest work, partly from the dark glow it acquires
through persistent rubbing by home-made beeswax and linseed
oil or, surprisingly, by a tallow candle. My chair with its cabriole
feet from a Queen Anne model and elaborate banister-splat
magnificently shows the glossy piebald wooding of the yew.
But making chairs from yew-wood is no joke, the worker
frequently suffering from migraine or dizziness on account of the
poisonous exhalations.

Mr. Goodchild takes his designs, modified for the occasions,
mostly from Sheraton, Hepplewhite, Windsor and Ladder-back
models between 1700 and 1780, and on the occasion of one visit

to him I made a truly romantic discovery. A dozen or so years ago I bought at Heal's a pair of "Gothic pattern" arm-chairs—chairs, that is to say, whose backs resemble one type of elliptic Decorated bar-tracery in fourteenth-century windows. He was showing me some of these backs and, one thing leading to another, I found out that he had been the maker of my Heal chairs. But his spirit is remote from that of the art student who sets an easel down before an old master in the National Gallery. He approaches his masters as a master himself in the tradition of English chair-making, an initiate by right of descent in the calling of a crafts-man. Nothing could better illustrate the datelessness of the old crafts than this inward continuity. Their association with the past is purely arbitrary; they are back numbers only because a barbar-ous age has no use for them. Country crafts can never be rightly understood except as being essentially independent of time. There was no reason in Nature, a natural love of beauty and human need why they should not have gone on for the duration of man's tenure of the earth, since the generations of craftsmen represent a chain of re-creation on the exact analogy of the poet's "Thou wast not born for death, immortal bird." Their virtual extermination in our own time has been sheer murder by an evil economics; it has nothing whatever to do with replace-ment or internal decay. Theirs has been an innocent death and the blood is on the head of the killer.

One interesting thing is the racial type of the great majority of survivors in the Chiltern crafts. They are presumed to have a gipsy strain in them, but I do not believe it. Nearly all of them are small, dark, lithe, supple, small-boned and long-headed, and this is Mediterranean, that is to say, Neolithic. Goodchild, Rockall, Saunders and others that I know all conform to this type, but this Neolithic persistence in the Chilterns has never been remarked. Yet it is both natural and reasonable to suppose that this race of fine craftsmen in flint and stone, certainly in touch with Medi-terranean culture, did not altogether perish. Maiden's Bower near Dunstable and the barrow on Whiteleaf were both definitely Neolithic in origin, while the forested hills first of oak and later of beech have been the refuge for outcast and oppressed from time immemorial. The predominance of hamlets over villages; the constellation of heaths and commons; the comparative insignificance of the towns; the very intricacy of the valley systems have been other factors favourable to the continuity of the Neolithic stock. I suspect that it became mixed with Danish rather than Saxon blood, and there is some reason for thinking that there was a Scandinavian settlement in the Turville area.

VI

Past and Present

Hughenden is a step nearer High Wycombe than any of the group just surveyed and its cedars and D'Israeli memorials have been so favourite a theme with the guide-books that they fortunately leave me little to say. The Park seems to me very dull and sad and the church hideous, though, as at Hambleden, roses climb over the flint wall of the nave. An emaciated fifteenth-century effigy in a tomb-recess under a plain canopy has its torso covered with initials, a grim comment on the fame of Hughenden.

The village is now part of Wycombe. A lane off the Princes Risborough road under high banks and trees whose roots clutch them in long knuckled fingers leads up past a group of bartons to the road called *Ridge Way*. Go not that deceiving way; it leads if not to the everlasting bonfire to as likely an earthly image of it as the country-lover will care to see. There is a view of the uplands flowing down to the Wycombe Valley unconscious of their fate. Struggle blindly east across the Amersham road and there is Penn, another famous place. Being on the watershed of the Wye and Misbourne rivers commanding a view of Windsor and the Thames Valley, it shows up those lurid contrasts between new and old, suburban and rural, which the places within the orbit of Wycombe so sharply manifest. The strung-out cottages, those that are left, are extremely individual examples of those happy variations in conformity with the native style which occur with minor differences at Bledlow, Checkendon, Turville and elsewhere. A cottage with a date-label of 1655 has dormers, rounded Dutch gables, brick dripstones and an ornamental brick frame with flint fillings. But the roof is slate, the very last material that should appear on an exposed ridge. Farther on, another has triangular dormers, another an elegant timber framing and a third a pyramidal porch. The contrast between these cottages of the country and the villas of the town among them is as acute as that between the cherry orchards on one side of the road and the villas on the other on the way to Penn from Hazlemere and from Hazlemere to Hughenden.

The contrasts of this region are indeed so numerous that its explorer passes on from the fact of them to varieties in them. Hatchards Lane is one, winding between low hills and linking up the nearer Wycombe area with the Kingshill plateau to the north. It alternates in the most abruptly disconcerting fashion between rurality and the suburban. Yet a basket-maker still

M

lingers there, and near Dean there is the further surprise of footpath notice-boards that are not the macabre emanations of
bureaucratic æsthetics. Great Kingshill on its enormous green
looks utterly incapable of any surprise, even "only a little one."
Sterile uniformity, sentimental stylelessness wipe out its identity,
and this nondescript character makes the labyrinth of inter-
crossing roads through a country and a soil (clay-with-flints),
dull at the best of times, a nightmare. You are turning here and
there, passing from road to road like a fly on a pane of glass and
all the time you are going from nowhere to nowhere. Is this not
what nightmare is? How intensely significant it is that this
destruction of rural individuality is exactly paralleled by recent
European developments in which personal character and integrity
are being submerged under mass-movements and a despotic
uniformity! We can never understand what twentieth-century
civilization really is without correlating all its phenomena.

Yet Great Kingshill springs a wonder—Wonder No. 2—that
in its way is just as overwhelming as though an angel took it upon
himself to trouble the polluted waters of the Wye between
Wycombe and Bourne End. It is so momentous a surprise that
without exaggeration it leaves the traveller gaping. In the very
centre of the ugliest, most featureless part of the village is a
cluster of ricks (96) belonging to the farm of Mr. Lisley
which exhibits some of the best workmanship in thatching that
ever I have seen, not merely in the Chilterns, which have a poor
tradition in thatch, but anywhere in England after years of
noticing differences in the techniques of local styles in rick-
thatching. These Lisley ricks are, as we say in Oxon, a "masterbit"
and as much superior to the average rick as a poem to a set of
newspaper verses. What is more, all the rounded ones have each
a "dolly" at the apex, a stylized crown of plaited straw sur-
mounted by a tuft of wheat ears and coiled at the base with a
woven straw-band which, as Mr. Lisley told me himself, is
30 feet long. A more eloquent example could not be of traditional
craftsmanship of the utmost finish and delicacy triumphing over
every obstacle, every discouragement and adversity. Mr. Lisley
told me that he could not sell his pigs and cattle at rates worth
their keep, that prices were worse than in the zero-year of 1938,
that the cost of imported cake and fodder was ruinous for a
small farmer—and he only has 90 acres. So much for "Home
Production" in a time of bitter need. In such circumstances and
in such a wilderness as Great Kingshill his tenacity in building,
thatching and decorating ricks of such quality is nothing short of
heroic.

95   THE ENTRANCE TO HAMPDEN PARK

96   FINISHING HAYSTACKS AT LISLEY'S FARM, GREAT KINGSHILL

97   SHACKS IN A CHALK VALLEY NEAR MARLOW

But it is more than heroic. Mr. Lisley's farm is a perfect example of mixed, family, traditional husbandry, properly balanced between arable and pasture and virtually self-subsistent until the artificial scarcity of labour compelled him to buy his winter fodder from abroad and a tractor to save his fields from going out of cultivation. Love and instinctive knowledge of the soil are inherent in such men, and mechanization is abhorrent to them because they know it to be a makeshift attempt to replace the essential human labour that has been driven off the land by the starvation of our agriculture in the financial interests of foreign importation. Farmers of this yeoman-peasant type are not deceived and exactly the same thing was told me by another farmer, a wise and genial man, at Weston Turville. He himself, round-faced, jolly, mild-spoken, shrewd and independent, is just the type which hates to see good arable tumbling down to weedy pasture, just the type in fact which was once the corner-stone and stay of England, just the type which understands that the new principles of bio-dynamic farming, the reverse of "scientific" forcing, make conscious the methods of cultivation which in their forefathers were instinctive. His grandfather was a notable thatcher of Seer Green in the Hundreds, so that he illustrated in his own person the axiom that the old-style peasant-farmer is naturally allied to the craftsman and that craftsmanship is kept alive in a period inimical to its survival by family inheritance.

It was therefore very gratifying to me that his son has not left his father's farm and inherits his craftsmanly faculty. This son, of the same racial type as Harold Goodchild, presented me with a model, 17 inches high by 22 inches round, of his father's ricks which he had made for the Harvest Festival of 1939. The straw was plaited upon a rounded wooden base, pyramidally sloped at the top, and is now one of the treasures of my museum. I cherish it not only because it is a fine specimen of peasant art, but because it is a symbolic tower—rich as any of those ivory towers and dark towers and pleasure-domes of literature—of the marriage between use and beauty which husbandry has joined together for thousands of years in the service of God and man.

I am going to say nothing about the course of the Wye with its string of paper-mills south-east from High Wycombe through Loudwater (83) right down to Bourne End, because there is nothing to say. It is a desert of modern industry, patched up in places with prettiness. Except geographically, it has nothing to do with the Chilterns.

VII

THE HAMPDENS AND THE HAMPDEN LEGEND

It seems queer that I should include the Hampden area in a survey of the Wycombe orbit, since it lies a mile or so north of the circumference of the arc of settlements already drawn and reveals only light traces of the shock of contrast between urban and rural which has branded them. My reason for including this area is a historical, not a topographical, one and to it I will come.

Grim's Dyke up from Lacey Green by Speen Bottom is the connecting link between the two regions, and a well-defined length of it can be seen in the wood by Redland End, south-west of Great Hampden. Even though it has a course of 16 miles in Bucks between Bradenham and Ashridge and the ramp is 40 feet wide and the fosse 30 feet deep in the best portions, it is the most elusive and mysterious earthwork of any of its kind in England, few of which are remarkable for candour. The boundary theory is vastly more probable than the defensive one. We usually jump for war in our speculations, not because the prehistoric age was particularly warlike but because the present one is so. Huxley, for instance, was sure that the primitive was a savage because he lived in the savage age of industrialism. It is impossible to grasp the meaning of a peaceful society when your own is the reverse of it. It is extremely unlikely that Grim's Dyke was a fortification because of its multiplicity of twists and turns and corners, because of its immense length (it is the longest serpent of antiquity) impossible among warring tribes and because the lower the ground the less developed are the works. A good point about it is that it is always near the watershed except where the latter rises above the scarp-line. It hardly ever leaves the woods and even at Nuffield is shadowed by beeches and even when a coil of it straightens out it quivers. Near the Pink and Lily Inn (where Rupert Brooke delighted to write doggerel verses about what "a free man may do"—but that was a long, long time ago), it approaches close to the scarp above Princes Risborough. But soon, python-like, it seeks the woods of the interior again. I fancy it may have been used as a hollow way for sheep and cattle between West Wycombe and Cholesbury Camps, but that idea does not conflict with its use as a boundary. Its enigma will never be solved and I am glad that it is free for ever of antiquarian jargons and of the totalitarian dogmas of Mr. O. G. S. Crawford.

I remember an autumn day in the Hampden region wonderfully in tone with the mystery of Grim's Dyke. The great woods swept fierily over the upheaved masses of Kop Hill, Pulpit Hill and Coombe Hill as though the sun had set on earth and the wooded hills were its clouds. The light over the plain from Kop Hill etched it out with a clarity that at the same time invested it with a delicate bloom, an effect of the rarest. Inland, the combination of bright sunshine with indigo-coloured clouds that sagged to earth in a kind of blue-black smoke and trees of burnished orange and golden bronze transported land and sky into a new world full of wildness, splendour and dark ecstasy. Out of the tawny stubble rose the field-fires, and drifts of white smoke, iridescent from the rays of the sun behind them, rose up to join the pendulous curtains of smoky cloud let down from above. Against this sombre background the trees leaped out into a blaze of supernatural intensity. If a great painter had witnessed such a scene, he would have despaired; he would have felt his utmost efforts, his furthest vision of glory on blade and leaf to have been a ghost of such reality in Nature. And indeed Nature herself was beyond herself, and past and present, the material and the transcendental, seemed to have met in an eternal moment both of wrath and of exultance. The thunders of Isaiah and the magical rapture of Vaughan the Silurist might be thought of as the language of such an apocalyptic scene, but in mortal speech they could not be juxtaposed as before my eyes the darkness intensified the light and the light gave depth to the dark.

To my mind the best of Hampden is not the mansion for all its bristling battlements nor the church nor the country, an undulant tableland and rather commonplace, nor the waves of the land to the west where the mistletoe grows generously on the boughs. It is the trees in the Park, the ancient limes and sweet chestnuts with ridged and spiralling bark, and the noble avenue as seen from the pepper-pot lodges (89) or half-way up the slope, where the two great wings of the double lines stretch out to the right hand and the left. How much finer that avenue looks to-day with the grass growing in the open nave between the arcaded columns than it could have done when it was a "carriage-way." Yet nothing in Great Hampden is so beautiful as Little Hampden to the north. One reason is the exquisitely chosen site of the church on its mound, looking on the one hand towards the long ridge of Hampdenleaf Wood, in front down to the farmstead group below, white-walled and red-roofed, and on the other hand to Little Hampden Common whose capping of brick earth makes this secret pocket of the hills uncommonly rich in vegetation. The beech lowers its Chiltern prerogative before the variety of its lusty neighbours, including the copper beech; orchises and helleborine, epipactis and habenaria and even the rare wintergreen are still part of the woodland flora, and the box, used in the Middle Ages to decorate the churches on Palm Sunday, grows dense and wild.

But the beauty of Little Hampden lies neither in the Common nor in the hamlet adjoining it nor in the swing of the valley south but in their trinity. At a glance it is seen how perfectly traditional cultivation fits into primeval nature. I may add the satisfaction of the scenic follow-through of the world within from the world without. The timbered and belfried fifteenth-century porch, itself harmonious in kind with the farm-buildings below the mound, admits the wayfarer, filled with good air and good sights, into a nave which is a gallery of wall paintings. They are very varied in theme—lions, a Weighing of Souls, with Our Lady, true to her traditional rôle of cheating the devil of his due by pulling down the scales, figures under trefoiled canopies and three St. Christophers—and cover three centuries from the thirteenth onwards. The pictorial association of these three primary elements at Little Hampden—religious mythology, husbandry and wild Nature—make it not only one of the most appealing but symbolic places of rest in all the Chilterns.

On the face of it, therefore, the Hampden country is immune from the Wycombe influence. Historically speaking, and here is the greatest contrast of all, what came out of Hampden was ultimately responsible for High Wycombe as it is to-day and for that unbalanced preponderance of urban over rural culture which has virtually extirpated the latter. This is a historical verity never mentioned in any book, whether of history or topography, whose subject is concerned with the Chilterns. On the contrary, these books unanimously make pilgrimage to Hampden as "the shrine of English liberties." The *Highways and Byways* volume indeed commits itself to the extraordinary statement that John Hampden "struck . . . a great blow for liberties that were never again to be in vital danger." An examination of this claim shows it to be a fallacy as widely diffused and destitute of supporting facts as the equally well-known scientific fallacy as to the pugnacity of primitive communities, and it is the business of later writers to examine it.

The follies and arbitrary measures of King Charles have no bearing whatever upon the issue in question, which is the actual consequences of the Puritan revolt and the Puritan victory. So far as country life is concerned, the Puritan suppression of

98 THE MAIN STREET AND TOWN HALL, AMERSHAM

rural liberties is beyond dispute. The rhythmic and communal gatherings of the peasants for celebrating the ancient rituals of seasonal husbandry were put down with an almost Teutonic harshness and severity, nor have they ever recovered from the blow struck at the heart of those free expressions of a chain of village communities far more democratic in their essential structure and traditions than the electoral democracy of to-day has even conceived. No democracy is more firmly based than when it is rooted in the ownership of land. The spirit of common rejoicing for the benefactions of earth, the living link between "holiday" and "holy day," the very musical soul of England were strangled for good and all by the intolerance of Puritan absolutism. The partiality of the Whig historians has conveniently forgotten that the Long Parliament went so far in the practice of tyranny as to abolish Christmas Day and its observance by worship with it. The liberty-lovers arrested John Evelyn for attending service on the supreme day of festival and gaoled a sea-captain for kissing his wife on a Sunday after an absence of three years.

But the effect of the Puritan Revolution in depressing English liberties had far wider implications and results than these. The masterly studies of R. H. Tawney in *The Agrarian Revolt in the Sixteenth Century* and *Religion and the Rise of Capitalism* have by the use of contemporary documents deeply incriminated the part played by Puritans in the enclosure of the common fields and the destruction of the fraternal liberties in right of free assembly, right of regulating the parochial affairs of the community and rights of ownership or usage in agricultural privileges. But the Cromwellian dictatorship, the bleak hostility of the Puritan ideal to the æsthetic and communal heritage of the peasant and its religious vandalism are still only incidentals. The kernel must be sought in Tawney's brilliant analysis of the association between Puritanism and the money-power. He reveals how the mental force of Puritanism was employed in breaking down the leavings of the mediæval restrictions against usury and economic self-interest, and he cites some astonishing extracts from contemporary Puritan "ideology" as witness of its successful attempt to segregate social morality from any control over economic relations. Calvin's "legitimacy of moderate interest" was expanded into a doctrine of success in business as "almost a sign of spiritual grace" until profit-making was interpreted as a positive duty and the invading hosts of economic appetites found in the Puritan the opener of the gates. When the social vices of one age emerged as the economic *and moral* virtues of another, there was no longer any check except lack of opportunity (and that was sound religion to overcome) to a boundless exploitation. The energies expressed in commercial enterprise were idealized by the special attachments of Puritan thought until covetousness was lifted up to be the righteous enemy of sloth, gaining the world became a means of salvation and the Christian synonymous with the "economic man."

Tawney's researches can leave no possible doubt that it was the Puritan party which divided ethics from economics and played a decisive part in the change-over from the conception of society as a spiritual organism to that of society as an economic machine. By the time of the Restoration, the "profligacy of the courtier was accompanied by the economic orgies of the Puritan merchant," and it was a Puritan who engineered the Dutch trade-war of 1665–7. Only through Tawney's powers of intellectual synthesis is it possible to understand why the horrors of the early factory system escaped moral reprobation from the most respectable and high-minded of politicians, economists and Cobdenite Liberals. In Tawney's word, "Compromise is impossible between the Church of Christ and the idolatry of wealth, which is the practical religion of capitalist societies, as it was between the Church and the State idolatry of the Roman Empire"—and, I may add, of modern Europe. The power of the Puritan Revolution lay in achieving that compromise and in closing the gap between religion and plutocracy. The Puritan served God *and* Mammon and ended by rendering to Mammon the things that were God's.

Since the Chilterns are so deeply associated with the Puritan Revolution, I propose to take the issue a little further than Tawney has done and by so doing bring it back to where I started from, namely, the historical relation between High Wycombe and Great Hampden. Tawney has hardly, I think, given sufficient prominence in his argument to the element of predestination in the Puritan thought, directly inherited from Calvin himself, and the legitimate father of the modern theory of progress. Mr. J. C. Hardwick in *Totalitarianism* has justly pointed out that the Darwinian theory was in itself "a kind of Calvinism." "The strong were predestined to push the weak to the wall, thus fulfilling the demands of Nature, and therefore of the Creator." But Darwinism—that great stimulus to a predatory commerce —was still more appositely the fulfilment of Puritanism, because it so perfectly squared with the doctrine of the "economic man" evolved by Puritanism. In time, the reaction against the unbridled exercise of economic power became centred in the gospel according to Karl Marx, and precisely the same elements of Puritan thought appear in him as had given his adversary control over the kingdoms of this world. Communism was predestined to take the place of capitalism by the Darwinian concept of inevitable progress, a concept from which the spiritual factor was rigidly excluded. It is because of the entire compatibility between Marxism and the idea of the mechanized State, supported by science and big business, that Russia and Germany are hand-in-hand to-day. Both have inherited the fully developed Puritan idea, as we in our turn inherit it by the channel of financial interests. And that this is not drawing a long bow is demonstrated by the Astor-Rowntree Report on British Agriculture, published in 1939, which at a time of supreme necessity for the rehabilitation of our agriculture discouraged the "domestic production of staple foods" lest it should interfere with our "international commercial policy," the very element which has been the prime cause of its decay—some would put it more strongly, of its ruin.

The last link in the chain of causation is the natural antithesis between the country with its ethic of self-sufficiency and the town with its drive of economic expediency from which sprang intensive urbanization, mechanization and the mass-production of goods. It was the Puritan who was the bridge in the transition from a rural to an urban England and thus it becomes apparent why Hampden, the seat of the county magnate who was among the first to take up arms against the King in the Civil War, comes in the relation of cause and effect within the orbit of High Wycombe, a typical example of a small market-town urbanized by modernity. It is only by blindness, ignorant or deliberate, to nine-tenths of the truth that such a place as Hampden can be regarded as "the shrine of English liberties."

A word as to Hampden himself. The author of *The Sun at Noon* (1939) records a very interesting conversation between Lucius Cary, Viscount Falkland, a truly great man who got himself killed in the Civil War because he was wise enough to perceive its ruinous folly, with Hampden on the eve of its outbreak. "He (Hampden)," said Falkland, "was full of pride, violence and acrimony of spirit" and declared that "very much blood must be spilt . . . and an entire conquest was necessary before peace could ever be made." Falkland's biographer makes it clear that Hampden had no affinity with moderate men like Sir Edward Verney on the King's side and Sir William Waller on the Parliamentary. It may be doubted whether a man is a hero

N

of liberty who in the interests of party and the refusal to pay the Government an unjust tax does not hesitate to plunge his country into fratricide. If his example had been generally followed, there would never have been even intervals of peace in the subsequent history of England.

100   THE WIDE MAIN STREET OF BEACONSFIELD, LOOKING WEST

102   THE WEST WING, SHARDELOES HOUSE
An early work of Robert Adam

101   A WOODLAND LANE IN SPRING, NEAR
JORDANS

VI

CONQUERED COUNTRY

I

SUBURBIA (92–4, 97, 114–115)

EXCEPT for most of the Hertfordshire Chilterns in the north-west between Ivinghoe and Hemel Hempstead and certain pockets to be particularized, the whole of the rest of the Chilterns from a line drawn between Hampden and Beaconsfield and thence north-eastward as far as the banks of the Colne has been suburbanized. What is this phenomenon—Suburbia—so familiar and so little analysed? It is, of course, the culmination of a historical process reaching back to the Industrial Revolution and beyond that to the series of causes which moved England to abandon the ideal of self-subsistence for that of economic expansion, a country life with market and cathedral towns as nuclei for an urban life with the country as parasitic upon it. The formidable list of country industries destroyed by the Revolution as given in Lord Ernle's *English Farming Past and Present* marks the earlier stages in this process of which Suburbia, so far as the country is concerned, is the last manifestation.

I have therefore to summarize in brief what that manifestation is. The essence of Suburbia is a paradox: it is distinguished by its lacks and not by its possessions, except in its possession of the country surveyed in this chapter. That conquest has been a positive achievement, and yet its qualities are oddly blank and negative. Its cultural qualifications are neutral because it is at once remote from the intellectual centralization of the towns and cut off from the profound and stable traditions of rural life. It has in fact deserted the town in order to betray the country. Living in the

country and working in the town, the suburban is neither nomad
nor settled, urban nor rural. He is sub-urban and nothing positive
nor creative can come out of a control of the country which
wears in its name and in its acts a subservience to the town.
Suburbia is a drifting thing; its aims are divided and its roots
aerial, and yet its yoke is fixed firm upon our English earth,
fixed too in the most throttling sense, since in the Chilterns it
sits upon tens of thousands of acres of fertile land, acutely
needed for the production of English food to feed English people.
It is for this reason, I think, that it is non-productive in character,
art and principle of life. In the average Suburbia, a Dorothy
Perkins prettiness is its only æsthetic ideal; its pleasures are
imitation-urban, its work largely parasitic. The places where it
settles become neither town nor country because itself remains
urban-minded within a rural environment. Mainly composed of
the upper or lower middle classes, it betrays the same indefinite-
ness in status (which often makes it pretentious and aggressive)
as in place, escaping from the town as it does and yet clinging
to it, loving the country and killing the thing it loves. It is not
at all malignant by nature and yet, wherever it goes, it expels
the native population, pulls down its cottages or puts them in
fancy-dress, builds houses of its own as characterless and innocent
of design as are all its acts, debases the neighbouring countryside
and suppresses its crafts and husbandry. It is thus destructive
with the best of intentions, and this is due to an amorphous body
finding itself in a false and anomalous position, lacking poise,
stability, rhythm. So far as the land is concerned, this new
population is purely ornamental just as its culture is, and it is
this hollowness within which is, to my thinking, responsible
for the real devastation it unknowingly and unthinkingly inflicts
upon the countryside. In victimizing the country it is itself
victimized by the predatory interests in building and real estate
which are strong and vigorous in purpose. Their motive is
purely egotistic; they know what they want and get it. Suburbia
is not at all like that: on the contrary it is full not of greed but of
sentiment. I do not myself believe it will ever become subdued
to what it lives on, because its nature is essentially paradoxical
and all its restlessness and uneasiness proceed from this building
on the sand. Only, I fear, some such cataclysm as the war or its
aftermath can restore to the countryside the reality of which
Suburbia has deprived it.

The Chess and Misbourne Valleys and the country between
their roughly parallel south-easterly courses—the first rising in
the uplands above Chesham and flowing into the Colne at

Rickmansworth, the second and southern river rising on the
Hampden plateau and joining the Colne at Denham—this inter-
fluvial terrain and a great square block of country north of the
Chess between Chesham on the west, Berkhamsted and Hemel
Hempstead over the Herts border in the north, Watford and
Rickmansworth in the east, all this country has been colonized
by Suburbia. It is Metroland. I do not mean to say that there is
no country left: there is plenty of it. I do not only mean that
it has become diluted, sentimentalized, picturesquified, de-
countrified—a peril to which its features were naturally vulner-

CORNFIELD NEAR PENN

able because of their more feminine cast than along the scarp-
line and farther south and west. I knew this country well many
years ago and its delicacy, almost fragility, of landscape was its
danger: it could not survive insensitive treatment. What I mean
is that it has been conquered by urban immigration and in the
process has taken on the character—or rather lack of it—of its
conquerors.

In such a country, a place like Palladian Shardeloes and its
park (102) and lake on the Misbourne, the home of the
Drake family which built Amersham Town Hall, sticks out like
a volcanic peak in the Pacific. Its strong, haughty, self-conscious,
rather bleak individuality is asserted in this now "mignon"

plaything kind of country with a withering contempt. Why? Because the identity of this part of the Chilterns has been obliterated, and the sure indication of what that means is that I, once familiar with it, can no longer find my way about it. I am always getting lost because every way is becoming more or less the same way. The hills are still there; the woods have not been all cut down, but they are now the "charming surroundings" of an advertisement in real estate. Local differentiation is no more. My companion on one such journey let the cat out of the bag. She said—somewhere between Chenies and Chalfont St. Giles— "Are we on the Chilterns now?" when, geographically speaking, we were slap in the middle of them. But she was right: we might have been anywhere, except in the country. It has become an anonymous land, a land that has lost its memory. So we asked the way again and again, and the answer always was, "I'm a stranger in these parts." I realized that everybody was a stranger in these parts, whatever parts they were. It was a country without a name as well as without natives; in a rather terrifying way it was depersonalized. That is what I mean by saying that the country has taken on the characteristics of its new settlers. The loss of the individual, whether in thing, place or person, is the danger to which our twentieth-century civilization has exposed the world, and in this sinister fashion the countryside of these Chilterns betrays it. One of the villas in these parts is called "Hill Vue." Yes, indeed, there are no views any more, only vues.

Therefore, it is not a land of violent contrasts—of beauty and ugliness cheek by cheek—as the country of the Wycombe orbit reveals. We now go looking for needles in bottles of hay, shards in a midden, fragments of identity, bits of definition, hidden under what is or what was called progress, which is a very polite way of putting it. We have to look under the bedside manner that tells the patient with flushed cheeks that he is getting better and better every day for symptoms of former health and truth—for things that go immemorially with the stooks and the sheaves and the bleached stubble on the gentle slopes cradling the baby Misbourne.

II

BY CHESS AND MISBOURNE

All the same, we are back at Amersham among the violent contrasts of the Wycombes. The way the street of the old

103 SARRATT CHURCH

104 THE GREEN AND MODEL COTTAGES, CHENIES

105-7 JORDANS: THE MEETING-HOUSE AND THE FRIENDS' GRAVES
Those of William and Gulielma Penn to the left

town, still virgin[1] (98, 99), takes the valley beside the Misbourne is a marvel of generous spacing and bold broad planning reconciled to the warm russet colouring, variety within certain limits, and comfortableness of traditional Chiltern architecture. Spaciousness and domesticity in one—it was a great achievement. Defoe called the effect of red brick and tile upon a jagged line of toy gables "very antical," and there is certainly an element of the marionette show in Chiltern buildings, dollish with odd corners and brisk improvisation in line. Many of the houses, including the belfried and arcaded Town Hall (98), the demure Almshouses, the Grammar School, the Swan Inn (99) and the King's Arms, restored with a very heavy hand, are of the seventeenth century, but periods jostle as do Dutch and Chiltern gables, Gothic and rural-classical, sash and casement windows, timbering and brick-work, and all with the greatest amity. Two great secrets of earth the old builders possessed, the gift of *siting* and the knowledge that it is unlikeness, not uniformity, that makes for concord. Each house contains those elements of balance, proportion and economy of structure which are the three essentials of the country crafts. We can no longer build country houses because we have killed out these qualities with the crafts.

There were burnings once at Amersham, and Baxter preached controversy there, but fanaticism did not prevent the folk from going on making harmonious and useful things as a matter of course. How has the charmer escaped with Amersham New Town next door? The only answer I can find is that the street was already so wide that even a County Council was impotent to distort it, and so it was spared the fate of Chalfont St. Peter to the south-east, which had the modern road driven through its entrails as in the old days a stake was driven through the heart of a malefactor.

How can a resident "in these parts" walk, as hundreds must do every day, from New to Old Town (which looks as though lace and straw-plait were still made there) next door without, I won't say self-horror, but discomfort and the sense of something wrong in the difference? Why do not sociologists investigate the causes that prevent the colonists of New Town from seeing the difference, and so repenting and by common agreement burning

[1] But since this line was written, the Town Council has pulled down its island block in the High Street which gave such a special character and meaning to its proportions, an act of vandalism parallel with that of the demolition of Bury St. Edmunds by yet another barbarian local bureaucracy. When such abominations as these are openly practised, what moral or æsthetic right have we to be outraged by the bombing of Canterbury and Bath by the barbarian enemy?

it? It is the business of sociology to find out. What will posterity say to those imitation Le Corbusier frights climbing the shoulders of the Misbourne Valley slope (93)? The people who built them and live in them are the people who say, "Whatever we do, we must not put the clock back." They need not be afraid that they will rediscover the eternal truths. As an old farmer of Edlesborough remarked, "If the new ways won't do, try the old 'uns again," but necessity, not sense, will drive that lesson home.

The Missendens higher up the stream are on the borders of the Bad Lands, that is to say, the unproductive lands in the fullest sense of the term. The bigger shows remains of its Georgian origin, including some decorative fanlights, has Grim's Dyke in Woodlands Park to the north-west, some fine sycamores and a church (with some early glass and another of those twelfth-century fonts of Chiltern home-make) placed above the small town or large village by one of those strokes of genius once as common as small beer. At Little Missenden, on a capping of clay-with-flints quite different from the alluvial of Great Missenden, there is old roughcast on the eighteenth-century fronts that stand among the week-end cottages. The Misbourne is crossed outside the village, a murmurous, furtive, shallow, child-like stream with bowed trees and meadows of roughage on either side. Its polished pebbles, its little noiseless noise among the leaves that overhang it, the millhouse there which was genuine up to 1914, console the traveller's weariness and tell him that all he has seen are the more ephemeral the falser they are to hill and vale. They will pass as the river itself passes on its way through the water-meadows.

Chalfont St. Giles, by the lower stream where it begins to issue from the dwarfish hills, dawns like the opening bars of a Mozart concerto, with green fields and a duck-pond. Dance-music soon breaks in, but enough of the original music is caught through the jargon to sketch out in retrospect strings of sixteenth-, seventeenth- and eighteenth-century houses looking at each other across a drawn-out green in that companionable way Chiltern cottages have with them. They once made pottery here and the kind of bricks of which was built Milton's "pretty box," as his friend, Ellwood, who is supposed to have suggested "Paradise Found" to him in 1665, called it, at the top end of the village. It is odd how these parts attracted poets, Puritans and politicians: perhaps their feminine graces were whisperings to the first, an escape from inhibitions to the second and relaxation to the third. Actually Milton came here to escape the plague which in the different form of ugliness (itself a kind of disease) has followed

108   THE SURVIVING PORTION, CHENIES MANOR HOUSE

109   ASHRIDGE HOUSE, A RANGE INCLUDING THE CHAPEL

110 A STRETCH OF THE COMMON, CHOLESBURY, ABOVE CHESHAM

111 THE RIVER GADE AT WATER END, NEAR HEMEL HEMPSTEAD

him three centuries later. The cottage, a hutch of thin timber framing with brick filling, casement windows and shouldered detached chimney, with the Fleetwood Arms on the front gable, is or was (for it has been messed about) pure Chiltern, especially in this region where flint is scarcer than out of it. It still has poetry in it, though of that silver lyrical spontaneous quality that is like the landscape rather than in the consciously grand manner of *Paradise Lost*. The church, reached through an admirable lych gate of old timber and a churchyard of hideous marble and granite crosses (a mid-Victorian invention) and headstones, has remarkable murals and Jacobean wood-work in it, quite apart from the tables of the Ten Commandments beside and above the chancel arch. These murals—one is of Salome turning cart-wheels before Herod—were the cinemas and B.B.C. talks of the Middle Ages, with this difference, that villages no longer instruct and entertain themselves (nor towns either) nor do workers make their own pictures and formulate their own programmes. When murals were painted, this is just what villages and villagers did do. As La Fontaine wisely remarked, "Si quelque affaire t'importe, ne la fais point par procureur!"

Sober Jordans (105–107) is near by, now built up but not indecently so. It is surely a mistake, by the way, to think of the Quakers in the same breath with the Presbyterians. They were a party which revolted from the iron despotism of the Presbyterian system.

The Chess was once the prettiest creature wandering like Wordsworth's Lucy past mills (how shameful that these mills are not grinding the local corn in a time of necessity like the present!) and under willows and past fat meads and among mazes of steep woody uplands like Celtic curvilinear designs on metal. It still does, but in the meantime it has been to town or rather the town has come to it and in an indescribable fashion it has lost its virginity. It is no longer rural; it has gone rustic; it has become a kept woman of leisure. Nobody would guess that at Chesham, Cobbett's "nice little town lying in a deep and narrow valley," anything of the primitive innocence remained. The cottages made of "brick noggs" (brick fillings in a wood frame) are now to be found only in hiding, and the orchards of "merries" (little black cherries) have been mostly felled for building, while there are few oaks there now that he said were 80 feet high. Chesham has had a noble unwritten history in the crafts because of its position as the node of five convergent valleys and the receiving station of scattered hamlets and farmsteads covering a wide area. The valleys in rich curves led out to various moated homesteads, a foundry and a chapel. Shoemakers were in force at Chesham; there were tanyards for which the bark of the oaks was stripped in spring, brew-houses and many workshops for chair making and wood-turning. Before the Industrial Revolution Chesham must have fulfilled the same function as did the walled "polis" of the Celtic hilltop "camp," a focus for exchange of produce and bartering of commodities between the market inside the walls and the rural population without. Nearly all the crafts have vanished or been subdivided and mechanized, that is to say, denatured. The control and free spirit of the craftsman have given place to the economic servitude and automatic drudgery of the machine-minder. Here is a true tale that gives the measure of the change. My friend, Mr. T. Hennell, on his way through the town enquired whereabouts he could find any bodgers in the woods. "You won't find any in the woods," was the reply, "they're mostly jobbing gardeners and we call it doing bad work." It was explained that bodgers not botchers were the end in view, namely chair-leg makers. "Oh, you'd better go to Wycombe. They're all chairopodists there."

But the traditions of Chesham have been too stubborn to be altogether stamped out. Good stuff is still turned out by the Toy Factory—breakfast-set trays, salt and pepper castors, egg-cups, marmalade containers, children's spades and what-not: they are expensive but still hand-made, though the power-lathe has supplanted the wheel-lathe. The wrought-iron work of J. F. and A. Gooding's smithy, again, is first-rate—door and cupboard fittings, hoes (including the swan-neck), blades, brand-tongs, pipe stoppers, spiral candlesticks mounted on horseshoes, candlesticks shaped like cup-and-saucer campanulas for a wall-bracket, post hinges for attachment to the harr of a field-gate, brackets for inn-signs and balling guns for shooting a pill down a horse's throat. From Gooding's I have in my museum an old "searcher-knife" with a raw-hide sheath for picking stones out of a horse's hoof. Chesham is still a son of its own motherland, broken as is its strength and crippled as are its powers—or this notice-board would not be seen to-day:

> NOTICE. Any person damaging these Greens or any part thereof, either by cutting the turf, Lighting fires, Pitching tents or Caravans, or otherwise, Depasturing, Horses, Cattle or Sheep, without having, Common Rights, so to do, WILL BE, PROSECUTED. By Order. CHESHAM. Lord of the Manor.

Chenies on its promontory above the Chess is down-stream past the toy waterfalls where Flaunden Bottom comes winding

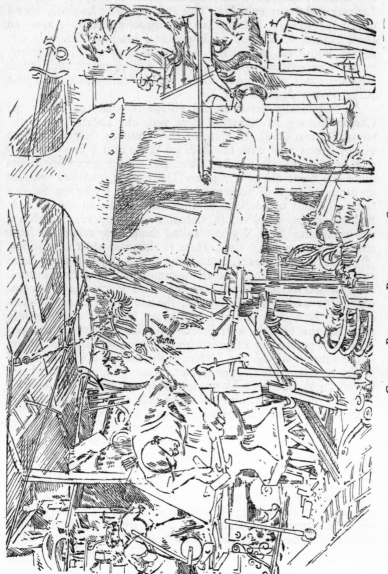

GOODING BROTHERS, BLACKSMITHS, CHESHAM

down under beechen walls from the north to Horace Walpole's
Latimer and the river valley. This soft, sensuous Latimer, once a
couch for Roman, Elizabethan, Georgian epicures, is now an
Ideal Homes Exhibition of bogus and beading. There is one
pigmy house of half-timber and brick with gables, dormers,
porch, casement windows and gently rolling russet roof which
represents this voluptuous corner with a felicity just short of a
Birket Fosterish sweetness.

An "idyllically rural" model village is what the books call
Chenies among its pollarded elms and, like Latimer, on a triangular green (104). In spite of this ominous description, the
village opens well with the Bedford Arms and a fine wrought-
iron bracket outside the Red Lion. But on the green bogus has
taken the heart out of the place. The church, restored without
an atom of taste or feeling, is only a shell, while the famous
sixteenth- and seventeenth-century monuments in the Russell-
Bedford chapel—"robed in alabaster and painted, cherubined
and seraphined," as Walpole called them—are railed off from
any but a skew-eyed view. Here is that turbulent, ambitious,
gifted, selfish aristocracy, patronizing the more florid arts, whose
struggle with the kings and the commoners of the land (natural
allies) ended so tragically for the latter and which was to become
mercantile under the Tudor and Puritan temptations. What a
contrast these chill splendid tombs are with the only moving
thing in the church, a fragment of stained glass in the east
window representing a figure with flowing gold hair, like an elm
in the autumn winds! The Manor, L-shaped and brick like others
in the region, with stepped gables, twisted chimneys and brick
turrets (108), had been as crudely over-restored as the church.
It is the dilapidated wing which is full of a haunting beauty
whereof our raw civilization knows nothing.

One last scene. Between the two rivers and in the heart of
Metroland to the east is a brick wilderness called Heronsgate.
It is the site of a Chartist land experiment in 1860 and all that is
left now is the name of one of the local pubs—"The Land of
Liberty." Chesterton who lived at Beaconsfield, Eric Gill who had
a printing press at High Wycombe, they might almost be called
the last not exactly of the Chartists but of those who have borne
on their standard the legend for which the Chartists implicitly
fought—"For England, Home and Beauty."

112 BERKHAMSTED CASTLE: THE KEEP FROM THE INNER MOAT

113 THE POND AND GREEN, ALDBURY, HERTFORDSHIRE

114, 115   BOWERDEAN FARM AND ITS VALLEY, NEAR BEACONSFIELD
As they were originally, and as they are after "Development"

III

THE HOUSE ON THE GREEN (94)

The rest of this country north of Chesham spreads in a great fan from Wendover to Watford. The guide-books are eloquent about its charms, but I came later in the dusk of their day. My sentiments about it are perfectly summed up in the title of Ford's play—*'Tis Pity She's a Whore*. The hill-village of Sarratt in the east, for instance, was called "very remote" and lots of other nice things. What does it matter now what shape its long green is, and who will visit its little Norman church with brick tower and saddleback (103) and a stalked Jacobean pulpit within for the love of humble and mellow country churches? Those who brave getting there through a country either ravished or sentimentalized will notice, not its likeness to a group of bartons (showing the immemorial recognition of how God loved the earth) but its estrangement from what is there to-day. The churchyard probably has more graveboards (there are more than twenty) than any other parish church in England. Bovingdon, on the crest of the watershed between Chess and Gade, was called "remote and unpeopled"; now it has ceased to exist. West of Chesham, you notice how the high-hedged twisty lanes of Hertfordshire have jumped over the border among the greens and heaths and holes and bottoms and scalloped ridges and hide-and-seek valleys of the Chilterns proper. Hyde Heath still has a woodturner; he has kept going by running a small engine. So you pass along like a sparrow picking up crumbs from a table that once was rich.

St. Leonard's, near Cholesbury, is a freakish whitewashed little chapel of the fifteenth century, restored in the seventeenth and with neo-Gothic windows of that period inserted. Under an aberrant roof are Gothicized furniture, a piscina-cum-sedilia in one, most curious, and a number of Renaissance and later tablets. Behind the periwig bust of Cornelius Wood, a soldier who died in 1712, is a whole arsenal of weapons and armour with acorns in carved wood and two cupids with gilt trumpets among them. Probably Nico Bogee, the sculptor, did not intend his Loves to make his War—Leonardo's *pazzia bestialissima*—look the pompous absurdity it does. This chapel has something elvish about it, which is more than can be said for Cholesbury, farther east, a huge green-common (110) with Grim's Dyke, a Celtic camp and notices of building sites upon it, and

P

Wigginton is a horrid church mid nasty houses in a splendid situation.

The key to all this country occurs on Commonwood Common between Sarratt and Chipperfield. Stretching right across in vast extension is one house (94). We counted ten gables of different shapes along the front, eight oriels, also variegated, and forty-five windows, all latticed if I remember aright. There was still plenty of room for what seemed an acre of fancy brick-work in different shades, a labyrinth of half-timbering, heavily pargetted plaster-work, yards and yards of highly-ornamental barge-boarding, mansarded roof-gables and an elevated wood of the tudorest of Tudor chimneys. It looked like seven Moreton Old Halls, as reconstructed at Hollywood, transhipped in segments, touched up in the Tottenham Court Road and then set in a row on Commonwood Common. At one end stood a fragment of what appeared to be the original building.

IV

"Happy, Homely Hertfordshire"

Fortunately, a glance at the wide area occupied by settlers who have forced a spiritual and material sterility upon its former fruitfulness is not the whole story. Parts of the Hertfordshire Chilterns are still honest country, though sadly deteriorated from what they were before the vested interests in imported cereals and cattle foods had knocked the bottom out of home production. The chalk of the Hertfordshire Chilterns is much overlaid by clayey and sandy loams, the reason for its mixed woodlands, the much smaller extent of monopolist beech-woods, the prevalence of the hornbeam and the predominance of arable over pasture. But artificially induced economic conditions have greatly decreased the oak-with-hornbeam woodlands and greatly increased the acreage of pasture lands which are nothing more than tumbled-down arable fields.

Between the Hertfordshire and Buckinghamshire Chilterns a buffer state is interposed, Ashridge, carved out of the spacious original Berkhamsted Common. Consequently, Skelton's Barcanstede Castle over the Bulbourne on the south is the true portal into this new land. The moated ruins show now as huge monoliths like those of the Grand Circle at Avebury (112), and conduct the mind back to their crowded feudal past from gavelkind to Gaveston, as the Adams doorways, half-timber overhangs

and cartsheds off the main road covering tumbrils and dung-
carts point to the past of Berkhamsted itself before it went bank-
rupt in beauty and rural service, which in the country mean the
same thing. Ashridge itself, into which the Common melts, is a
queer place. Thorn, gorse, bracken, birch, oak, hornbeam,
sycamore, conifers and noble beeches say one thing; the many
glades and turf rides, the litter baskets under the trees, the
notice-boards, the trimmings and that sensational house of
whitewash with a Reckitts blue pantile roof, say another. Ashridge is not really a Park; it is the fruit of a marriage of con-
venience between a piece of wild nature surviving from the
rich prehistoric Chiltern forests and an urban recreation ground,
and the result is a kind of imitation New Forest, with more trees
and less scrub.

But Ashridge House is a queerer. It was erected on the Bon-
hommes monastic foundation by the notorious James Wyatt,
"the Destroyer" who sacked the interior of Salisbury Cathedral,
in 1806–13, and was finished by his nephew. Even though you
may see it at a distance, say through the long avenue from the
Column of the crusty Duke of Bridgewater, it makes you blink.
The Quennells in *A History of Everyday Things in England* (Vol. III.)
admirably described it as "like a snowman, built up by sticking
on lumps instead of having good bones inside it." In my eyes,
its fortuitous eruption of white spires and towers and pinnacles
and battlements and cupolas and cloisters and buttresses and
acres of wall make it look like a gigantic wedding-cake, built
to celebrate the marriage aforementioned (109). It is absurd to
denominate so large-hearted a design by any one style, even
nineteenth-century neo-Gothic. It is an amalgam of that with
Florentine-Morisco-Tudor. Not that I approach it with any
repugnance. After the eastern Chilterns, which cannot be regarded
by any lover of England except with an extreme bitterness of
soul, it is an entertainment, and God knows we have little enough
of that in these days. It is hideous but it is also comic, is well
hidden among the trees and does no harm, even though they
did make a bonfire of the old furniture. A pleasanter thing in
Ashridge—because it can be admired—is the old ice-house
(also mentioned by the Quennells in their most readable book),
a kind of mighty well into which ice from the ponds was lowered,
built into the hillside, vaulted with brick and made a vacuum by
sloping doors and a vaulted passage. Taking into account the
kind of food we are forced to eat nowadays by our suicidal
refusal to call upon English land to bear any but a small per-
centage of the food the English eat, I am very interested in the

subject, and also in noting how much our ancestors accomplished with hand and brain without the use of machines that deprive us of both.

Ashridge is an anomaly, but that is just the reason why it should be crossed to reach the Valley of the Gade and its neighbourhood rather than by the entrances on either side at Tring and Hemel Hempstead. This valley and its heights are, though Chiltern country, a variation upon the rest of it, whether the freer south and west or the conquered east and north, and so should be penetrated by the bridge of the "Park" and not abruptly. What are the differences over and above those of general aspect already jotted? For one thing the Hertfordshire Chilterns are scant of woodland, if the setting of Aldbury (113), close to the scarp-edge, be excepted. Flint is less and colour-wash more conspicuous. Except at Nettleden where the landscape is boxed up as it is in the Flaunden region, the ridges do not squeeze in the valleys so tightly. The Saxon lanes, that twist and turn and double like the curling tendrils of Leonardo's drawing of Leda's hair at Wilton, the tilted cornfields that come down to them and the knots and groves of trees that boss the hillsides are more abundant than across the border into Bucks. This country is indeed transitory between the flatter and more open chalk ridges passing Hitchin and Baldock to the north-east and the shaggier, more crumpled type with its intricate mesh of valleys and bottoms to the south-west. And definitely it is more rural, much more so, and so authentic and not prettified. Only where the Valley of the Gade, that once washed out the footsteps of palæolithic man, makes by Water End (111) and Piccotts End to watery Hemel Hempstead, does that detestable mixture of rawness and sentimentality take over the scene. On the other side of the old town, now gashed by arterial roads and hacked to bits by tenth-rate building, the country changes back at once to the Chenies type.

Aldbury, inland from the gap of the Pitstone and Ivinghoe Hills, lays its head and tail in easy accommodation to the large directing curve of the wooded hills above. The tail is flattened by the terracing of the slopes with warm dormered brick-houses, one with a seventeenth-century hipped roof. Broken lengths, round conical stacks and seventeenth-century Almshouses of thatch, weatherboarding, brick, tile and plaster lead willing feet to the green on the horn of the curve (113) with its elm and pond and stocks and flint-towered church. Meadows in the foreground gentle the approach to the hills. Layout was half the secret of the old builders, and outskirt building has in consequence scribbled over the set of nine-tenths of the villages of England. Aldbury has escaped this brutish insensibility and is thus one of the very rarest villages in all the Chilterns.

Nettleden to the east with its pale grey and yellow-washed brick houses has a further association with the Bucks Chilterns in its brick church, but the continuity of the ridges between it and the Gaddesdens to the north is free of the fussiness that bothers the surveyor of the Bucks chalk hills across the Gade. By Little Gaddesden, the semi-wooded range swings out into a long bare promontory like a hand held in blessing over the plain. Great Gaddesden, that stretches almost at full length down a steep hillside facing the Gade, varies its brick fronts with much timbering and some roughcast. The gracious church with its Decorated windows stands half-way down by some farm buildings, and a village church should if possible always stand by a farm that the saying may be fulfilled—man shall not live by bread alone, with its corollary that bread-growing and bread-making should be the foundation of his life. Across the river and the water-meadows the valley-ridge with twin swellings like breasts flows gently away. I turned with reluctance to the squat tower with its stair-turret peering well above it. But it was worth it. Within, the tie-beams of the roof are upheld by corbels of bold and fearless angels with heraldic shields, pleated robes, open wings and serene faces. Let them be my last written memory of the Chiltern Hills, whose beauty of nature and of husbandry will, long after I am dead, return and have these angels as of old to bless them with their outspread wings. Now they are but antiquities, with nothing to say to a century which has been the parricide of its past.

COPPICE IN WOOD: OAK, ASH, HAZEL AND BLACKTHORN

INDEX

HAMPDEN WOODS

INDEX

(The numerals in heavy type refer to the *figure numbers* of illustrations)

117